How To
Draw
Anything

To Pat for her support.

How To
Draw
Anything

by

Mark Linley

A HOW TO BOOK

ROBINSON

ROBINSON

First published in Great Britain in 1995
Material in this book has been drawn from *The Right Way to Draw*,
The Right Way to Draw People, *The Right Way to Draw Landscapes*,
The Right Way to Draw Animals and *The Right Way to Draw Cartoons*.

This edition published in 2015 by Robinson

A CIP catalogue record for this book
is available from the British Library.

ISBN: 978-0-71602-223-7 (paperback)
ISBN: 978-0-71602-331-9 (ebook)

Printed and bound in Great Britain by Clays Ltd, St Ives plc

Papers used by Robinson are from well-managed forests
and other responsible sources

MIX
Paper from
responsible sources
FSC
www.fsc.org   FSC® C104740

Robinson
An imprint of
Little, Brown Book Group
Carmelite House
50 Victoria Embankment
London EC4Y 0DZ

An Hachette UK Company
www.hachette.co.uk

www.littlebrown.co.uk

NOTE: The material contained in this book is set out in good faith for general
guidance and no liability can be accepted for loss or expense incurred as a result
of relying in particular circumstances on statements made in the book. Laws and
regulations are complex and liable to change, and readers should check the current
position with relevant authorities before making personal arrangements.

How To Books are published by Robinson, an imprint of Little, Brown Book Group. We
welcome proposals from authors who have first-hand experience of their subjects. Please
set out the aims of your book, its target market and its suggested contents in an email
to Nikki.Read@howtobooks.co.uk

Contents

1
You Can Learn To Draw

Yes, you really can! Many people think that learning to draw is difficult if not impossible. In fact, it need not be. If would-be artists treated the subject as fun and went about it in the right way, it could be possible for nearly everyone, like learning to drive. At first it may seem hard, but it isn't if the basic instruction is correct.

Once you have discovered how to draw landscapes, animals, people, cartoons and all the other things in this book, you should have no problem at all managing with any subject.

Expect mistakes

When tackling any new skill it is common sense to expect and accept that lots of mistakes will be made. It's part of the learning process. It is not unusual for students with no previous experience of draughtsmanship suddenly to discover that they can put down accurately what they see. It requires just three things for this to happen:

1. The ability to look properly
2. Self-confidence
3. The capacity to remember and carry out basic instructions.

You have the touch

I have not mentioned skill with pencil, pen or brush. The reason is because all who can write their names, already have sufficient touch and control to make a multitude of complex shapes – called the English alphabet. There are no harder lines, in nature, to record.

A semi-illiterate navvy with scarred, calloused, insensitive hands and a tendency to drink too many pints might start off at a disadvantage. But there are talented handicapped artists with no fingers who can draw; some use their feet, or mouths.

7

Think positive

Folks who learn quickly are often those who have enthusiasm for their subject and self-confidence. The way we think is vitally important to the way we operate. Many of us are brain-washed from childhood into thinking negatively about some things. We have all heard others say, for example, "I can't draw a straight line." When this is thought or said it becomes a command to the human computer, the sub-conscious mind, which then obeys the instruction by programming the individual to this end. "I can't" is then a barrier for as long as it is thought.

Think negatively and you will be programmed to do exactly what you have thought. You will never be able to control a pencil or pen well enough to put down the lines you see. You won't be able to observe shapes accurately, or define texture, and, of course, it will be your own fault.

Fig. 1 Yes, you really *can* learn to draw!

You have bought this book, so you are probably already a positive thinker; if not, you will be from now on. How do you do this? Very easy, just think and say, "I can learn to do anything" then forget about it. How long will it take? About a tenth of a split second or faster. What's more you can apply this simple rule to any subject for the rest of your life. You will have no barrier to stop you moving forward. It may encourage you to know that I am a self-taught artist.

8

Gifted?

I believe the term 'gifted' is too lightly used in respect of artists. Only one in every million or so can be truly said to be gifted. The rest of us are craftsmen with different degrees of skill. If you can write your name then you have enough touch to learn to draw. If asked to write an A, G, R or K you could do it without thinking. Well, within these pages you will not be called upon to draw anything harder than that. Most lines in nature are gently curved, wavy, or straight; even those that appear complicated at first are not if examined closely.

This is why it is vitally important for us artists to look properly at what we want to record. If our drawing goes wrong it is always because our looking was at fault, If, for example, you draw your spouse with a broken nose, cauliflower ears and crossed eyes when in fact the features are more or less normal, then your viewing is wrong or your humour wicked. If your sketch of the family moggy turns out to resemble a furry crocodile then you haven't focused correctly, or need glasses.

Looking properly is important and will be touched upon again, frequently, later in the book.

2
Start With Landscapes

All the drawings you do from this book should be bigger than the printed version.

What to use

Black-and-white drawings have a special charm and power. Indeed, before colour printing was invented, most illustrations were in this medium. Black ink and various nibs used to be common, but today artists use ready-made pens. All the drawings in this book were done with them. There is a huge range to choose from. I find that a small selection of pens, graded 0.1, 0.5, and 0.7, is more than adequate for most illustrations, and suggest that you purchase the same. Figure 3 will give you an idea of what to look for. Figure 4 shows examples of the widths of line these different sized pens produce. Despite being "throw away" pens they are made to

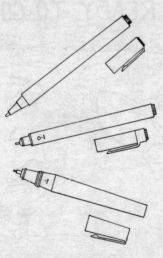

Fig. 3 Drawing pens.

10

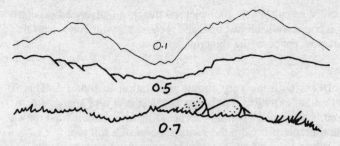

Fig. 4 Different line thicknesses.

give long service. One pen will contain enough black ink to make dozens of drawings. And they are not expensive.

A soft eraser is necessary. The person who makes no mistakes makes nothing!

Drawing pencils, graded 2B and 4B, are ideal for sketches. A size A4 cartridge drawing pad, or good quality typing paper – which is cheaper to buy by the ream – should enable you to get going. After you have gained a little experience you could add a small paint brush (number 3, 4 or 5) and a bottle of black drawing ink for blocking in large areas.

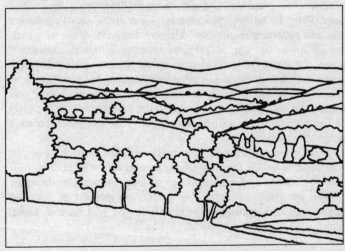

Fig. 5 An extended landscape.

Generally, though, the outlay on gear for drawing is much lower than for other art mediums. The satisfaction you will receive from this hobby will be worth many times more than the money spent. When your pictures reach an advanced standard you could well sell just one, and recover all your costs. Isn't that a happy, encouraging thought?

Off you go

Begin with the very simple illustration in figure 5. This is called an 'extended' landscape because it covers a large area of land. I happened upon this scene while on a ramble, and took a photograph of it from the vantage point of a hill top.

When you sit at a table in your kitchen-cum-studio, or wherever you decide to produce your masterpieces, a drawing board is useful. A purpose-made artists' board is expensive but strong plywood or chipboard is fine. I use a 50cm by 50cm piece of chipboard both for drawing and watercolour painting. One end I prop up to give a sloping surface, which helps the eye and makes drawing easier. Two hefty books do the job.

Churn them out

Some amateur artists believe they're doing well if they turn out three or four drawings in a week, but this is almost useless as a way to learn to draw. The more you draw the better you become. It's possible, and not hard, to draw ten subjects per hour. Prior to writing this chapter I wandered slowly round a zoo and recorded twenty six different subjects, some of which are in this book. The actual time spent on this was under two hours. One two-hour session in an art gallery produced forty quick sketches of people. This is not unusual for someone who can draw. It might seem difficult for a beginner, but if you follow the instructions given and do the assignments at the ends of the chapters you will be amazed at your progress, creative output and genius.

Always put the date on your work. When you look back you will be able to see the improvement, and this will bolster your self-confidence and enable you to go from strength to strength.

You are about to begin your adventure into art by drawing landscapes and learning what materials you will require. Good luck.

Fill in the white paper

Illustrators and artists need to know how to fill a blank sheet of paper. This is done both with the lines of the drawing and with shading. The latter marks are used to suggest different forms, distance and so on. Use the most simple of shading for

Fig. 6 Simple shading.

your first few exercises. Look at figure 6. Notice how distant patches of forest, hedges, and trees are recorded by vertical, even-spaced fine lines; how the field in the foreground is drawn with horizontal shading. Meadows further away are suggested by broken lines and small dashes. Trees in the foreground are made to look darker by a trick-of-the-trade often used, known as cross-hatching: diagonal lines are crossed at right-angles by similar diagonal lines going the opposite way. Grass is shown as little lines, dots and dashes. Go over your pencil out-line of figure 5/6 with a pen. Then rub out the pencil marks. Isn't it easy? You could do this with one eye closed!

Next, go to figure 7, which is a scene on the Isle of Wight. Take a long, careful *look* then draw in pencil.

Much of our U.K. countryside, incidentally, is inhabited by sheep. I always used to think of them as silly, nervous animals. However, when I was once sketching in the Yorkshire dales, an angry one with horns chased me. It must have gone mad. I finished up racing my friend to a stone stile where we climbed over to safety, but not before my friend had hurt her ankle. The sheep depicted in figure 7 are in the middle distance. They look like small oblongs with rounded ends. No detail is visible from a distance.

Figure 8 shows you how to shade in figure 7. Simplicity is the keynote again. However, the shading used for the trees in the foreground is slightly more advanced than in your previous sketch. Those trees to the left are partly cross-hatched, to help

13

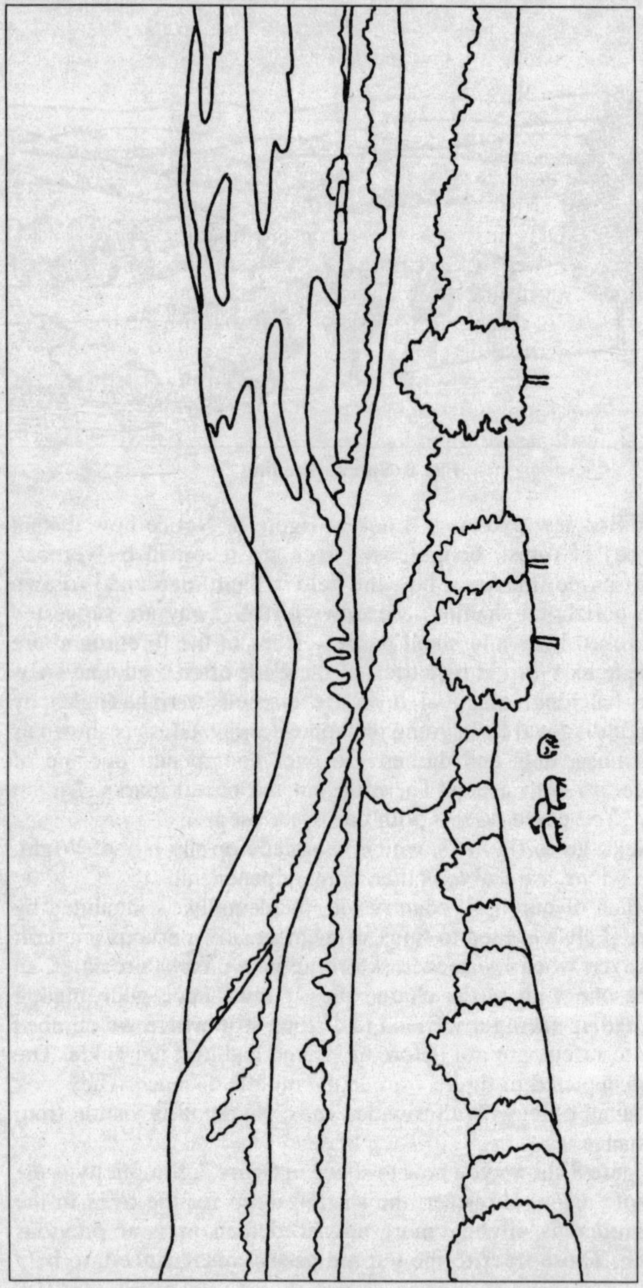

Fig. 7 Isle of Wight scene.

give a feeling of depth to the field. The ones in the middle are fully cross-hatched, with the addition of some simple squiggles. The effect of this extra shading is to bring these trees forward in the picture, towards your eye. Try it.

Simplification

Beginner artists tend to try to include every detail of what they see. This is impossible! Who has the time to spend a month drawing one tree? You can leave exact copying to a camera. What you must aim to do is simplify what you want to draw. Indeed, one of the highest forms of art is that in which detail is left out, the artist suggesting what things are like with as-few lines as possible. You have a lot of freedom. You can remove unwanted trees or buildings, change the way a river runs, or put in features that will improve a picture.

You are learning step-by-step the quickest way to reach a very high level of skill. Don't try too hard to produce identical copies of my drawings. That is not important at this stage. I want you to develop your own style. You can use your own ideas about how to create shading. We are all different, and express ourselves in our own, unique, way. One of my aims is to teach you basic drawing and shading, so that when you unleash yourself on, for example, the highlands of Scotland, you will know how to draw any scene that captures your attention. It would be very frustrating to sit before a breathtaking scene, pen poised over pad, and not know what to do!

Look for pictures as you go about your daily toil. Think how things could be simplified. We often take for granted those scenes with which we live constantly. When you take your spouse, children, or dog for a walk look around for pictures. If you glide off to work in your chauffeured Rolls-Royce take a squint at the countryside you are passing. The top of a bus is a good place from which to scan your environment. Parks, pretty gardens, golf courses, and all kinds of other local beauty spots will provide possible pictures. Part of being an artist is knowing how to *look*.

Practice makes perfect

The more you draw the better you become. We all know that, but success requires self-discipline too! We tend to take the easy way out (and expect to succeed without putting in the drawing hours...) but this works against us when learning a skill like drawing. It's interesting to know, however, that when newcomers begin to show good results their drawing tends

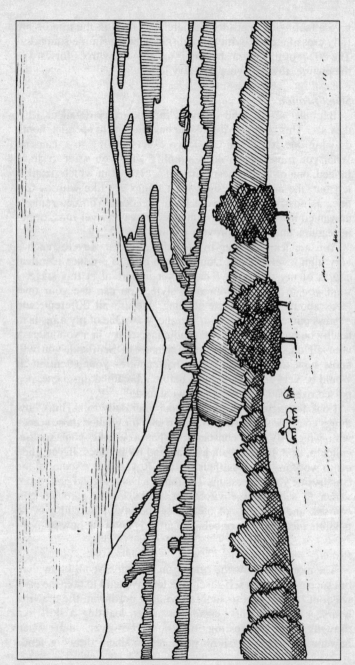

Fig. 8 More advanced shading.

quickly to become pleasantly addictive. I hope this will soon apply to you. Keep a small sketch pad with you and force yourself to draw scenes within easy reach. If you can't get about use photographs, old Christmas, or greetings cards, and so on.

Fig. 9 A roadside sketch.

Another step forward

So far all the pictures I have suggested you do have been very simple, and probably not worth framing. Very soon, however, you will make progress. Your first masterpiece is not far away! Aim to create an eye-catching gem, which will hang on your kitchen wall. It will become the talking point for all visitors. You know the sort of thing: "I did this from the top of Snowdon. We went there to exercise my bad leg but I couldn't resist dashing off a quickie of the wonderful scene below me!"

Next step ahead

Figure 9 is an outline sketch, drawn from a roadside in Scotland. Draw this either straight off with a pen, or lightly in pencil. Figure 10 is the same scene shaded and completed. Notice how thin, close lines are used to break up the white area of the sky. Leaves are suggested on the near trees, then lightly shaded over by diagonal lines. A few extra lines denote clefts in the rock in the foreground. The lines used for grass are more detailed near the artist, but they fade into dots and dashes further away. Now finish your picture in a similar fashion.

The final illustration in this chapter, figure 11, is the most advanced one in this section. It has been drawn in stages. Figures

Fig. 10 Shaded in.

12 and 13 show how you *must* set the scene with the outlines before you can tackle the detail. They should make it simple for you to copy figure 11. What more could you want? A drink? Very well then, but don't hang about too long; we have a lot to do!

Making a landscape drawing is a construction job. Different parts may be put together, but all sketches are built. Examine figure 11. Then start to copy this as in figure 12 – which is stage one of this construction. Use a size 0.5 pen to draw the mountains, near the river bank, and the large rocks. Notice how much blank paper there is to fill as you define your outlines.

Stage two, in figure 13, shows how a little more major detail is added. Now you have a few ripples to indicate water, broken outlines of trees in the foothills and more detail in the boulders and the single fir tree. Put the changes in with the same pen.

Return to figure 11 to complete the sketch. Change to your size 0.1 pen. Draw the sky lines first, then the distant trees and the shading on the hills. Your next task is to shade in the middle banks, followed by the boulders. Fine cracks on the rocks and the small wavy lines in the water are the last for you to tackle. You have now finished your most advanced picture. Congratulations! You are on your way.

Shading, with a little practice, should be done rapidly. To go fast is better. It helps to cut down errors because there isn't time to worry about, or doubt, your ability. Just allow your computer

Fig. 11 A slightly more advanced drawing.

(brain) to work for you. Be bold and confident. Ignore minor mistakes; indeed, expect them and take them in your stride.

By now you will know that ink illustrations take time and patience rather than a great talent. Artists find time to improve their crafts. I am sure you will do the same now you have joined our ranks.

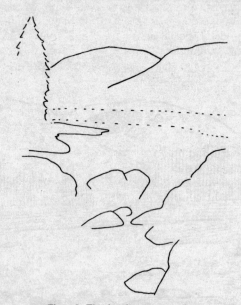

Fig. 12 The basic construction.

Fig. 13 A little more added.

By the way, there are as many, if not more, winter scenes drawn by artists as there are produced in other seasons. I think the countryside is special at any time, but – please forgive my bias – I must admit that sketching in warm sunshine beats standing knee-deep in slush in an icy force ten gale!

Important points
1. Be confident and bold.
2. *Look* and *look* again.
3. Be pleased with your progress.

3
Don't Rush Your Bridges

Bridges are a common feature of our countryside, and they are often used by artists as the centre-piece of a landscape picture. I shall show you how to obtain the effect of rock and stone, and give you an idea of how a bridge is constructed. Whenever you come across a nice looking bridge don't rush across it.

Loiter with intent

Walk around, under, and over the bridge. Try to fathom how the builders put it together. Did they use local materials? Is it an ancient structure? Who uses it? Would it make a good picture?

Examine figure 15. The top sketch is of a bridge in the Yorkshire Dales. Large slabs of local stone were used for the central arch. Stone and rocks, set in mortar, form the sides and are topped by big ridge stones. In this illustration each stone has been separately drawn. Notice how the builders used large rocks as part of the base, and thin ones around the arch. It's easy to draw. Have a shot at it.

The middle illustration is of a quite different structure. This is a fairly new bridge on the Linn of Dee, Scotland. When I visited this beautiful place I was impressed by the way designers had come up with a modern idea which fitted into the surroundings so well. Natural rock was used for the buttresses of the bridge and perfectly cut rectangular stones for the sides.

Copy this sketch. You have to pre-draw the straight lines in pencil with a rule. Small dots and dashes suggest the texture of rock.

The bottom drawing is of an ancient pack-horse bridge. There are still many of these lovely relics in our countryside. This bridge is an example of wonderful craftsmanship. See how tightly each rock fits into the whole design. No mortar was used. It's rather like dry stone walling in construction. The men who built it must have had a talent for jig-saw puzzles!

A tip worth remembering, when drawing walls, bridges, and

Fig. 15 Different structures.

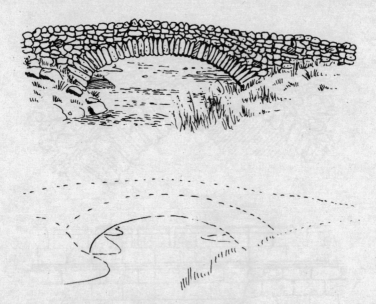

Fig. 16 The ancient pack-horse bridge at Wantendlath.

some buildings, is that it isn't necessary exactly to copy each individual rock or stone. This would take ages to do. Although each piece will need to be drawn individually, the best way is to decide what shapes the material has, and then draw *similar* shapes. In this bridge you can see that tooth-like rocks were used for the arch, while many different-sized stones went into the sides.

A 0.1 size pen was used for these illustrations. Now you can try them. Draw each stone and rock separately. Put in a few cracks and lines, and there you are – finished. Wasn't it easy?

Fig. 17 A peckish pony.

Fig. 18 Wantendlath Bridge from the opposite side.

Fig. 19 Start with a pencil sketch.

Your first little gem

I have used Wantendlath bridge for figure 16. This old pack-horse bridge straddles a stream which comes from a tarn at the foot of impressive hills. Wantendlath is a hamlet of small cottages and farm buildings which nestles between steep rocky mountains. I drew the structure with no background detail. One very hot summer day I sat on a large boulder to draw this picture. A pony took an interest in the event. He was feeling peckish, and raided my bag for salad sandwiches and an apple. (Figure 17.) All was not lost though! There was a tea shop handy so it was my lucky day!

Look at the lower sketch in figure 16; then copy this in pencil. When you are satisfied with your outlines, complete the drawing with a 0.1 size pen to match the top illustration. See how stones, grass, and water have been suggested. There is nothing too difficult for you to manage.

The next sketch of the same bridge was taken from the opposite side for figure 18. Now it's time for you to create your first masterpiece for the kitchen wall. Figure 19 shows you how to make the basic drawing in pencil. Once this is right you can begin to draw in ink your finest picture to date.

First, put in the sky lines with a 0.1 pen. Next add the distant hill line and then the main bridge construction. Leave all shading and details until last. Draw in the stone shapes one-by-one, but leave two small gaps on the bridge for where tufts of grass have grown. Put in the five bar gate. Flesh out, almost black, the fir trees.

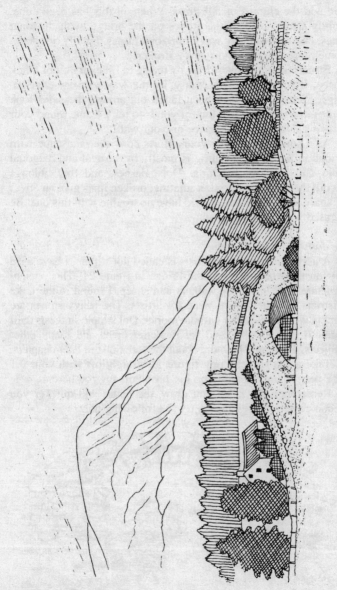

Fig. 20 Landscape with bridge.

Now you can shade in the rocks, the underside of the bridge, and add the clumps of tall grass. When all this has been done, lightly shade some of the stones on the bridge, with diagonal lines. Portray water by wavy horizontal lines. Finally, jot down some more grass by short spiky strokes.

Be careful not to over-draw by trying to fill every bit of blank space. It isn't always necessary, by the way, to draw edge-to-edge. Pictures that have been faded out around the sides look quite attractive. The last job for you is to ink a frame round your drawing. Now choose a space on your wall!

As a small reward for your efforts copy the landscape with bridge in figure 20. Shading is mostly by vertical and diagonal lines and by cross-hatching. Dots, dashes, and tiny oblongs record the bridge material. Radiating, broken lines give an effect of space in the sky. You should have no trouble with this one. Be pleased with your progress.

Be dotty

A useful technique for artists is called dot stipple. I have used this on the stone work on the bridge in figure 21. This ancient structure, still in use by walkers and sheep, I found in the Lake District – another super place for artists. The heavy stones are simply wedged together without mortar. Dot stipple suggests their form. It can also be used for depicting trees and many other subjects. There will be more about the technique in later chapters.

Take a challenge! Copy figure 21 straight off with your 0.1 size pen. Again, there are no big problems for you here.

Remember, the more you draw, the better and quicker you become. Before pressing on try the following quiz.

Fig. 21 Use dots for effect.

Quiz
1. How would you tackle drawing a bridge?
2. Give a tip about drawing bridges.
3. How is grass shown?
4. What technique is good for rough stone?

Answers
1. Study it from *all* angles.
2. Don't try to draw each stone.
3. By short lines or dashes.
4. Dot stipple.

4
Tangle With Timber

Today, perhaps more than ever before, we have discovered how important trees are to life on our planet. Trees provide food, medicine, organic material for the soil, oxygen for the atmosphere. They prevent erosion, give shelter, balance nature, and can transform a barren area. Each mature tree is a wild-life city. Birds, animals and insects abound. When chopped down – in minutes with a chain saw – the timber has many uses.

Trees are a joy to our eyes and they refresh our spirits. When I visit my favourite forest, the Wyre, to the surprise of any companion who might be with me, I talk to the trees. "Hello! It's nice to see you again," I say. My enthusiasm for trees, wild places and creatures dates from childhood. I like to feel that I can be part of the scene when I am let loose!

Get to know trees

The more you know about the subjects that you want to draw, the easier it is for you to refine the detail. As you can guess, it boils down to having a good *look* first. So far you have drawn trees in a simple way. Now I shall show you how to depict trees with added realism. In many landscape pictures trees tend to be in the middle or far distance. They can be handled on the simple lines learned hitherto. However, where a tree is the main foreground subject in an illustration, then in order to draw it accurately you need to know how to obtain the detailed effects of bark, branches, and foliage.

What problems must you solve? First ask yourself what shape the tree is. Is it round, tall, or spread out? What do the leaves look like? Are they fine, broad, pointed, or odd shaped? What is the bark like? Smooth, craggy, ridged, ringed, or what? As with all subjects, it is essential constantly to re-examine the construction of the items that go into a picture.

Figure 22 illustrates how to depict foliage, trunk, and branches. Notice how dark shadows help to give the trees depth and form. The top drawing, a maple tree, has been shaded on one

Fig. 22 How to suggest foliage.

side and almost blocked out where the deep shadows are. A few small, fine pen strokes were used to suggest the grain of the bark.

The two trees in the middle were shaded after they were drawn, with light, short strokes. These were cross-hatched to give deep shadows.

The bottom sketches were deliberately enlarged to show you how to make your foliage.

Fig. 23 A controlled scribble.

Copy all these trees in pencil. Then go over your work with a size 0.1 pen. There are no great difficulties for you. You don't have to use the identical shapes or shading which I have used. You may prefer to express your own ideas of how to obtain similar results. You could easily become the best tree artist in the whole world. I hope that you do!

Control your scribble

Figure 23 is comprised of a variety of trees and bushes drawn in the same manner experienced artists would use on work to be published or exhibited. How is it done? Answer, very easily! The effect of leaves and shadows to make up the sort of tree drawn in figure 23 is created by what I call a controlled scribble. *After* the main tree shape has been drawn with fine, dotted pencil lines (later to be erased), this outline is then filled by controlled scribble. Hold your pen fairly loosely. Obtain the desired effect by making quick, small twirls, circles, squiggles, wiggles, dots and dashes. Produce deep, dark shadows with white bits showing through to give a sense of texture and form. With just a little practice it really is easy to do. The finished result is very professional. Now try your own scribble!

Winter trees

After the leaves have fallen in winter, we can clearly see how a tree is constructed, and how one differs from another. Look at the elm, at the top of figure 24. See how different it is from the poplar, birch and fir on the same page. Patience and good observation are required to draw a winter tree accurately. Once again you must ask yourself exactly what it is you see. What shape is the tree or bush? Which way do its branches grow – up, out, or down? What are the twigs like? How does the bark appear – ridged, wrinkled, or smooth?

The best way to start your drawing of a winter tree is with an outline shape. I then move to the trunk, follow by putting in main branches and, last of all, add the twigs. The only problem with this kind of picture is that it takes time, but any attractive drawing is well worth a small slice of our precious life. Besides, it keeps us off the streets!

Trees to the front

Artists frequently use trees as a focal point in a picture. Figure 25 shows how a group of fir trees on an island has been used in the foreground to give an idea of the scale of the mountains beyond. Copy this drawing. Start with the sky lines to suggest cloud movement there, then sketch in the hills, followed by the island and the tall trees. The band of middle-distance trees is portrayed with a controlled scribble. The same technique is applied to the bushes on the island. The fir branches are suggested by masses of two, three or four short strokes drawn with a fine pen. Notice how some of these point upwards,

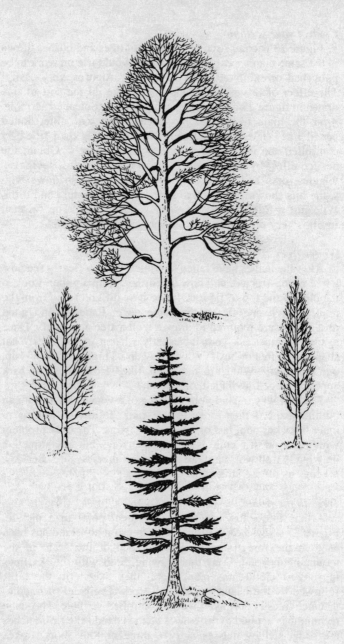

Fig. 24 Trees in winter.

34

Fig. 25 Trees in the foreground.

while others go downwards. The portrayal of water is obtained by wavy, horizontal dashes as in previous work. This little picture could be another one for your kitchen wall. If, by some remote chance, your masterpiece isn't quite up to your expectations give it away to someone you don't much like!

How is your bark?

For a good tree to be featured as the main subject of a picture you must know how to produce realistic looking bark. Figure 26, drawn in one of my local parks, shows four types of bark. The beautiful silver birch tree is a popular subject for landscape work, and is simple to draw. See how the white trunk is marred by triangular black blotches which increase in number towards the base of the tree. The bark surface pattern is shown by curved lines which run around the trunk. The branches are dark in tone and this is shown by shading.

The trunk of a fir tree is quite different. The bark is made up of large over-lapping scales which appear to hang down the tree. Each of these slate-like pieces, when viewed close up, can be seen to have small flakes in its make up. I have depicted them with a few fine lines.

35

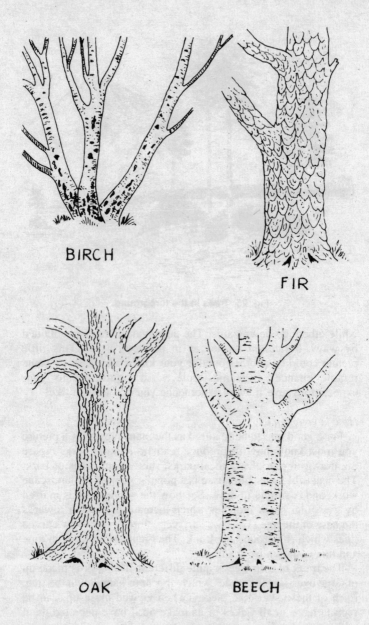

BIRCH

FIR

OAK

BEECH

Fig. 26 Tree trunk detail.

Fig. 27 Scribbled bushes.

The common oak, often drawn or painted by artists, is nice to sketch. The bark is composed of rough, deep ridges, with many cracks and crannies. These trees have heavy, sometimes twisted, branches.

A point to remember, with trees, is to draw one side in shadow, with markings more detailed than the opposite side. This helps to create depth and shape. If you use the same way of depicting bark for the whole trunk, it will look flat. Make one side lighter, with less detail.

The beech tree is another common tree which is fine to draw. The bark lines go around the trunk and are smooth compared to those of the oak.

See how the roots are suggested on the different trees in figure 26.

Copy all the drawings straight off with a size 0.1 pen.

Go behind the bushes

It pays to spend a bit of time behind the bushes, in the name of art of course! Figure 27 illustrates how bushes and small shrubs are drawn. Well executed, they are attractive parts of a picture. Notice how the scribbled dense shadows tend to project the lighter parts and this helps to suggest the form of a bush. Trunks and branches are only partly seen. Copy the examples in figure 27. Doing them will give you more practice with your scribble.

Assignments

1. Draw your nearest tree.
2. Draw the trunks of four different trees.
3. Look at some bushes and then draw them with a controlled scribble.
4. Examine the foliage of a tree in the distance. Then draw the tree.

5

Take To The Hills

You should have gained some skill in sketching rocks and stone in Chapter 3, Don't Rush Your Bridges. Your experience will now be extended. I will show you how to draw the huge boulders and rocks which feature in many mountain scenes.

The island of Skye, for me, has the most wonderful mountain range in our country. The Lake District and the Scottish Highlands come a close equal second. I will, however, for this chapter take you, via sketches, mainly on a visit to one of the majestic peaks of the Black Cuillin mountains of Skye. My drawings began on a visit when I once clambered up there on a hot summer day.

Rocks and boulders simply drawn

Take a look at figure 28. The top illustration is of a cairn which is a heap of stones made to way-mark mountain walks. (They may have been used for other purposes in years past.) This particular one was in the Lake District. Notice the vertical lines and the cross-hatching used to depict shadow. The middle drawing shows boulders drawn very simply. Fine lines suggest cracks, splits and texture. The bottom sketch is of rock slabs with small ridges and cracks. Heavy infilling is used for the darkest parts. These are all easy drawing jobs. Copy them all. Then move on to figure 29.

The new technique here is one for shading clouds. They are best outlined lightly in pencil; then you use a pen to put in the sky lines round the fluffy shapes; finally you erase the pencil outlines. Go on to shade your mountain. Use cross-hatching to make deep shadow. The rocks in the foreground show well in contrast to the mountains beyond. I'm sure you will find this another easy exercise to do.

Figure 30 takes you a step further on. It has a similar cloud and sky effect, but the mountains contain slightly more shading than those in previous sketches. Lots of little lines were used in a kind of controlled scribble. The sea is suggested by horizontal

Fig. 28 Rocks and boulders – simply drawn.

lines. The reflection of the lowest hill, nearest the sea, is depicted by wavy ones. Copy this picture.

Figure 31 has dark-looking mountains which are easy to draw. The dense areas were obtained with cross-hatching. After sketching this example in ink, you may care to draw it again in

Fig. 29 An easy exercise.

Fig. 30 Lots of little lines used.

Fig. 31 An easily drawn dark mountain range.

pencil or using a coloured crayon. It is useful to increase the range of your artistic skill. Each medium brings a different majesty to the picture. Try them and see!

Interesting rock structures

On a walk on the Island of Skye I came across a beautiful bay. Seals swam in sparkling blue water; sea-birds filled the air with their cries. The rock formation in the bay, shown in figure 32, was fascinating. I climbed up onto the shelf-like part, but could go no higher without a rope or a helper. The rock structure was buff-coloured, and it had several kinds of texture. There were slabs, boulders, splits, and pebble size projections, all of which were hard on hands, knees and shins.

Figure 33 is of the basic shape of this ancient natural architecture. Draw the outline in pencil then proceed in ink as in figure 32. This illustration took me around an hour to complete after I had the outline in place. I started with the sky lines, then moved on to the dot stipple on the high point of the rock. I worked slowly down to the deep shadow under the shelf, and then suggested with fine lines the lava layers in the base. There are no great difficulties. Just take your time. Your copy will be one to treasure.

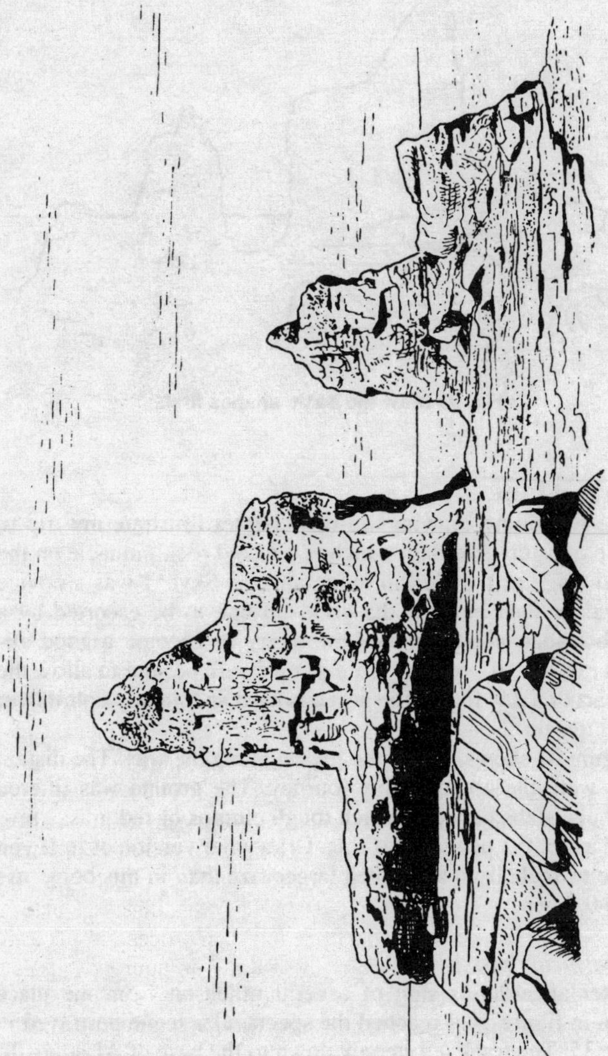

Fig. 32 An interesting structure.

Fig. 33 Draw the basic shapes first.

A trip to the top

The remaining drawings in this chapter illustrate my trip to the top of Sgurr Alasdair, which is a naked rock pinnacle on the central ridge of the Cuillin mountains on Skye. I was a novice hill-walker then but had the good fortune to be escorted by a superb leader who prompted me to try to become a good all-round rambler. If you ever attempt this walk be sure to allow the best part of a day for it. The going is hard and mostly uphill over varied terrain.

Figure 34 shows part of the region along the way. The distant peaks were the object of my journey. The ground was littered with huge slabs between which tough clumps of red grass grew. I used a size 0.1 pen to draw this. Draw your version of it. If you decide to scale it up to a much larger size than in this book, use a size 0.5 pen.

Awe-inspiring peaks

After an arduous slog of several miles on from the place shown in figure 34, I reached the spectacular scene portrayed in figure 35. The track led steeply down to the base of Alasdair. To give you an idea of the immense size of its awe-inspiring peaks I have put two figures in. The small boulders higher up, recorded by dots, were knee high! The larger ones were taller than a house, with the odd one as high as a cathedral!

Fig. 34 A varied terrain.

The white path in the centre of the picture is called the Great Stone Chute which is a very apt name for it. Highly experienced mountaineers (and a few foolhardy novices like me) use this to descend quickly. The idea is to make a dash for it over the stony surface. This causes a carpet of quite large stones to propel you onwards. You feel as if you are being whisked down with the speed of an express train. Having a crack at it was one of the most exciting experiences of my life. I have heard that the record time taken for this very steep drop is eleven seconds. This feat I can assure you is hardly one challenged by the sane!

The route to the top is to the left of the chute. Many of the boulders are too big to climb over, so the going is slow. However, the views from the top are truly magnificent and worth all the hard effort.

For *your* hardest challenge to date draw this scene. It's much easier to sketch than it is to climb! Be prepared to spend two hours or more on this picture. Start with a pencil drawing. Then just keep plugging away. I shall leave you to examine the drawing and work out how I have done the shading as part of your study of how to portray mountainous terrain. If your attention does flag stop for a break. Stroke your cat, dog, or spouse. Have a coffee. Then resume your masterpiece for the lounge wall.

On top of the world

A view from the top of the Cuillin ridge is featured in figure 36. The dark grey peaks stood out against a shining sea and a blue sky. Distant shore and island disappeared into a heat haze. After the last exercise, drawing this illustration will be child's play for you.

Quiz
1. What is the best way to fill in deep shadow?
2. What is infilling useful for?
3. What would you use dot stipple for?
4. Fine lines are good for what?

Fig. 35 Awe inspiring peaks.

Fig. 36 A view from the top of Alasdair.

Answers
1. Cross-hatching or heavy infilling.
2. Trees, bushes, vegetation, distant mountains, rocks.
3. Stone, trees, bushes, rocks, and many other subjects.
4. Fine details of all kinds.

6
Buildings In Landscapes

Self-discipline

Different artists have different pet subjects. It could be that you don't have much enthusiasm for drawing buildings, but it is important to be self-disciplined in order to become skilled. To want to devote all your attention to your chosen subject is quite natural. This, however, tends to work against you in the long term. I state this from experience. For years I put my energy into becoming a reasonably good wildlife artist to the exclusion of other subjects. The net result was that, although my animals and birds were quite good, the backgrounds to my pictures were not of an equal standard. My people drawings in the early years also left a lot to be desired.

It pays to tackle all subjects in a professional way. The skill required, for example, to draw buildings accurately is just the same as that needed for drawing trees, animals, people, or whatever. All problems of draftsmanship are related. It is only the way we think about them that varies.

I have had students who, at first, shunned drawing a certain subject, only to find out after trying, that what was feared proved to be that at which they were best! Learn to draw *everything* well. Then you can specialise...

Start with basic construction lines

You are about to learn how to draw some of the buildings which crop up in landscapes. At this point in the book I won't worry you about the theories of perspective. There will be more about them in a later chapter. Obtaining the correct angle of slope in a roof, or the slanting lines of a building, is mostly a matter of good observation to experienced artists. You will learn to apply such experience as you progress.

The old barn used for figure 37 is in Northamptonshire. The way that the big stones had been used in the low wall and sides interested me. The end walls of red brick contrasted with the natural material. I wondered if the builder had run out of stone.

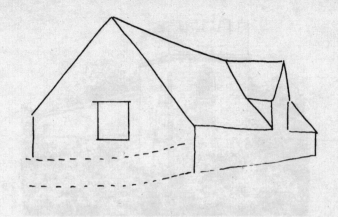

Fig. 37 An old farm building.

Copy this illustration by first putting down the main
construction lines as shown. Position this book and your piece
of paper beside each other. With the book held steady in one
hand, lay your pencil or pen lengthwise along the main ridge of
the roof with the other hand. Then transfer the same angle your
drawing instrument is laying at across the book over to your
piece of paper. Just shift the pen or pencil across and draw. Do
the same for the other angled lines and slopes. Doing this will
give you information about perspective. I used dot stipple to
denote texture in the large rocks. The ivy-covered tree was
added for interest.

Fig. 38 Clapham Church (Yorkshire).

Drawing sloping lines from life correctly is very nearly as easy. Simply hold up your pen or pencil between you and the line you are after, matching the angle, and transfer that line down onto your masterpiece.

A walk in the English countryside often reveals the tower of a church poking up through trees. Churches are very useful landmarks. They are shown on all good maps. Ramblers can

Fig. 39 Ruins are easy to draw.

check that their walk is on course by correctly locating a church. Old churches are especially nice to draw. Look at figure 38. Draw this and note how one side of the building has been shaded. The humble dot and dash is a wonderful device for artists. Here, they achieve the impression of stone, with ease. You will see that the trees and bushes were drawn using the same technique described in Chapter 4. This church should be easy for you to copy.

Old ruins are simple to draw and quite interesting to see. The heap of rocks in figure 39 is all that remains of a castle in the Yorkshire Dales. Sheep follow everywhere; I put in two to give a sense of scale. A copy of this example should take about half an hour. Off you go!

Fig. 40 A windmill that is easy to draw.

Variety is good

There are many types of building scattered around our countryside. The ones that are totally different from modern town dwellings are often the most interesting for us to sketch. Windmills, for instance, are not normally found next to the supermarket in the high street! Flat country such as in Holland, or the English Fens, is a better place to look for them. Figure 40 shows the way a windmill can dominate land it stands on. This particular specimen is both round and tapered. Draw the outline in pencil first. Make sure your basic lines are right before completing it in ink.

Figure 41 gives an example of a mill in the Cotswolds at a place called Lower Slaughter. How did it get a name like that? There is a resident artist in this hamlet who earns his living by producing paintings of the beautiful cottages found there. Good luck to him! I should like you to draw the mill in figure 41. There is slightly more to this one, but nothing beyond your powers. Start with a pencil sketch of the main building. Put in an outline of the mill wheel, the stone wall and the shed. Make sure you are happy with the overall proportions before you turn to ink. Notice the way the roofs come together, and how the

Fig. 41 A Cotswold mill and stream.

Fig. 42 A stone-built old building.

Fig. 43 A Yorkshire hill farm.

Fig. 44 A farm in the hills.

wheel has been treated. The stone work, trees, grass and water
are drawn as in other exercises you have already successfully
done. I have deliberately left out both sky lines and clouds. I
want you to do them in your own way. Your finished picture
may merit a frame; it's up to you.

I visited another hamlet to draw the building in figure 42.
This one is in the Lake District. I am not sure if it was once a
barn, stable or cottage. The dark grey stone used in the
construction seemed to me to be the same as that seen in the
hills overlooking this scene. I drew the stones separately. Then
I shaded with diagonal lines over the ones drawn in the end wall.
This gives shadow and so suggests depth. The shrubs and the
tree were produced with a controlled scribble. Draw this and
pop in a few clouds just for practice.

Farm buildings

Modern farms with water towers, stock sheds and massive
barns are not always very pleasant to see. Many old farms are also

spoilt for the viewer by rusty sheds and black-painted corrugated sheet barns. There are, however, still a few traditional farms about. I found the one shown in figure 43 up in the Yorkshire Dales. I sat on a plastic bag to draw this lovely scene. I did not include a pile of rocks and an unsightly shed in my picture. My original sketch was only 13cm across. I used a size 0.1 pen. The dry stone wall in the foreground was made up with many different sized stones of various shades. The wooden gate just about hung together and it tilted at an angle to the wall. The house was small with white-painted walls. There were tall clumps of reddish grass sprouting from the swampy ground and, of course, the "inevitable" sheep. The distant hills and patchwork of fields gave a sense of space and freedom. Copy this illustration.

Figure 44 shows farm buildings set against a background of hills. Dot stipple seemed the obvious way to suggest the large areas of scree (loose stones). Draw this example; it could be

Fig. 45 Sheep shelter and bridge.

another little gem for your hall, along with the sheep shelter and bridge shown in figure 45. The latter small drawing is a good example of dot stipple work.

In Wales and Scotland you sometimes come across a stone built cottage of the sort illustrated in figure 46. I expect these picturesque dwellings are hard to live in if you are used to the creature-comforts of a town house. They are, however, a

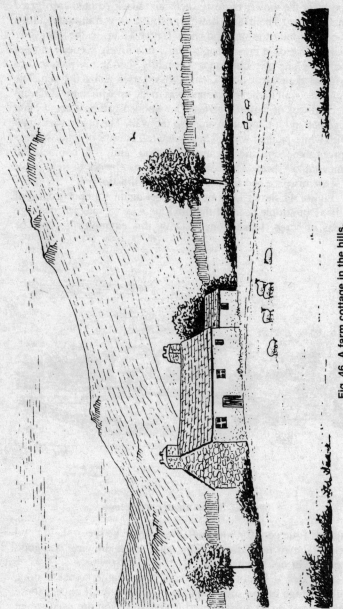

Fig. 46 A farm cottage in the hills.

Fig. 47 How to draw the thatch.

delightful feature for the landscape artist. A cottage set against a background of impressive hills like the example in figure 46 should by now be straightforward for you to copy.

Thatched cottages

Many people dream of owning a thatched cottage. These old buildings are part of our English heritage. They are lovely to look at, though I suspect not necessarily very practical to live in! There are several ways of drawing thatch. I prefer to create the image with tiny dashes which follow the slope of the roof. You cannot attempt to draw individual reeds. The result would be a mess! Notice in figure 47 how I have left areas of light to highlight the thatch. Copy this cottage.

Quiz
1. What is your first task in drawing a landscape?
2. How should you start?
3. What is the main problem in drawing buildings?
4. Which drawing techniques are useful for them?

Answers
1. Take a long, good *look*.
2. With a basic outline sketch.
3. Getting the slopes right (perspective).
4. Dots and dashes, controlled scribble, fine lines, shading.

7

Off To The Seaside

You deserve a nice break! So, in this chapter, we are off to the seaside. You may, like me, enjoy a spot of beachcombing or a romp along windswept shores. Some folk find their idea of heaven on a crowded beach but the reverse is true for me and, I suspect, for most artists; our joy is to sketch rolling waves, sunny sands or majestic cliffs.

After all your practice on landscapes, you already have the ability to draw a good seascape! The techniques for your pen are essentially the same.

Look for light and dark

An attractive seashore scene may, at first glance, seem to contain very little. Figure 49 is an example. There are two jagged rocks, a line of distant cliffs and a few gulls. Breakers with ever decreasing waves lap over wet sand which reflects the rock shapes. There is a pale sun which sets off an unusual pattern of clouds.

Drawing this picture was quite easy. I began with a line for the horizon and then put in the rocks. I gave these substance by using plenty of cross-hatching but I was careful to leave the rock edges bare. This was to show where sunlight was reflected. Waves and breakers I formed by using different thicknesses of line. I made extensive use of wavy lines, dashes, and dots, and created seaweed with a controlled scribble.

Your one new problem with this drawing might be the gulls. Look carefully at these. Note the rough oval shape of the body with a neck that can stretch or contract. The beak is short and slightly curved at the tip. The eyes are set fairly high in the head. I used light shading to distinguish the grey wings and the back of the birds in the sun. See where the light and dark areas are. But note the different treatment of the birds in the shadow of the rock. Now copy this illustration with a size 0.1 pen.

The methods for figure 49 apply equally to figure 50, a solitary figure on a shore. I drew this human quite simply.

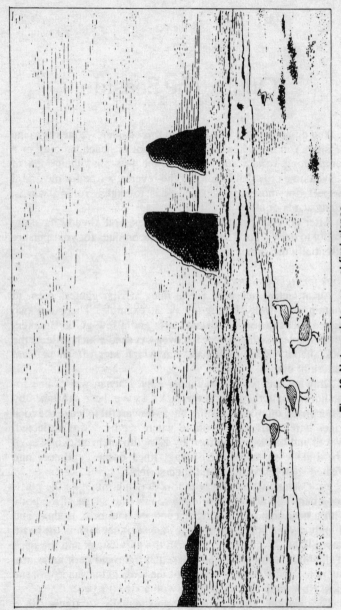

Fig. 49 Not much to see – at first glance.

Fig. 50 A solitary figure on a shore.

Figures of this kind are often used to add a little interest to pictures. They don't need much detail. I included the girl to give an impression of freedom, and space. Notice the way she walks into the scene rather than out of it. This is an important composition point. You want your viewer to look into and around your masterpieces, so design them with this in mind. I will return to this aspect later on.

If you have no experience at figure drawing try a few quick pencil sketches before you start with pen work. Then have a go at this illustration.

Learn from the masters

We can all learn from master-artists, both past and present. We can study their work and try to fathom how they achieved different effects. Sometimes we are even lucky enough to visit the places and look for ourselves at the scenes which were the subjects of their drawings. Not so long ago I visited the beautiful little island of Guernsey to follow in the footsteps of Auguste Renoir. The famous French Impressionist painter once made a trip there and painted sixteen or seventeen canvases in

Fig. 51 The bay Renoir painted.

just over three weeks. A hundred years later that event was celebrated by the issue of postage stamps showing some of those wonderful masterpieces.

I re-enlisted the help of my friend (of the Yorkshire sheep incident in Chapter 2) and off we went in search of Renoir's scenes. My chum is quite brilliant at reading maps. We quickly found our way to Moulin Huet Bay. By studying the stamps, we were able to locate the exact place where I thought the famous artist must have worked. I popped into a handy tea shop set in densely-wooded steep cliffs, and enquired about the illustrious visitor. The charming proprietor turned out to be a Member of Parliament for the island. His family and their ancestors owned the land Renoir visited. The precise spot from where one masterpiece was painted was on their back lawn. The tea was lovely, and the view marvellous. It was another lucky day!

The bay and cliffs were the same as they were in the French painter's day, but you could no longer see them from quite the same angle. Trees had grown and partly obscured the scene down below. We walked down a steep and narrow path to sea level. Maybe Renoir, who was quite old when he made his visit, could not manage this jaunt. I found the bay very interesting. Figure 51 is my drawing of Moulin Huet. It may not be worth quite the same as a Renoir oil (about 24 million dollars), but 'tis mine own!

Let's examine more closely my drawing of this bay from where Renoir painted several pictures. The heavily-wooded cliff top, you will see, is drawn by dot stipple, lots of it, and it does take time. Again, I purposely added a human figure to give an idea of scale. Just be patient copying this drawing.

Figure 52 is of a huge rock in the same bay. This was one of the subjects featured in Renoir's paintings. For an ink drawing it becomes a useful study of dark and light. I employed dense cross-hatching on the deeply shadowed side of the rock, vertical lines to shade the jagged headland in the distance and small dashes for ripples on the sea. A few patches of seaweed and three gulls were easy to add in order to complete this simple scene. I produced both of these drawings to a small scale with a size 0.1 pen. It will help you if you can make yours twice as big.

Fig. 52 Draw this huge rock.

Mess about with boats

If you love marine pictures you are going to want to draw boats. We shall mess about a bit with them here. Look at those shown in figure 53. The shape of their hulls is always pretty much the same even though there are so many different boat designs.

As the west shore of Guernsey has many natural little harbours formed amongst the jagged reefs, I was able to find a splendid array of types to draw for you.

Notice that masts on sailing boats are never dead centre; they are set forward towards the bow (the sharp end). On bigger yachts there is often a secondary mast near the stern (the blunt end). It will help you to draw a boat accurately if you imagine its hull shape as fitting into a box. Figure 54 illustrates what I mean. This technique is an aid to getting the dreaded perspective right. The canal long boat in figure 55 is an interesting vessel which reveals how its lines must diminish (come closer together) as they go back in distance away from you.

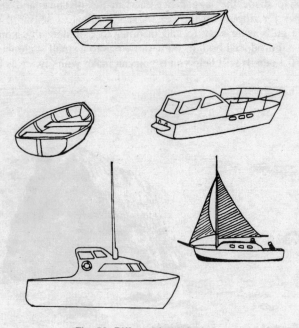

Fig. 53 Different boat designs.

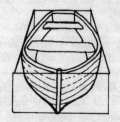

Fig. 54 Box your boat.

Fig. 55 Copy this canal boat.

Fig. 56 A fishing boat simply drawn.

Draw all the boats in figures 53, 54 and 55, before going on to figure 56. This is a simple study of a fishing boat on the shore. Fishing boats at rest are one of my favourite subjects. This one should be easy for you to copy.

The scene in figure 57 is a little more ambitious, but just as straightforward to draw. It shows one of the many natural mini-harbours on Guernsey. I have put in two small wader birds in the foreground and a contemplative figure at the edge of the sea. The diagonal sky lines suggest space and wind movement. The

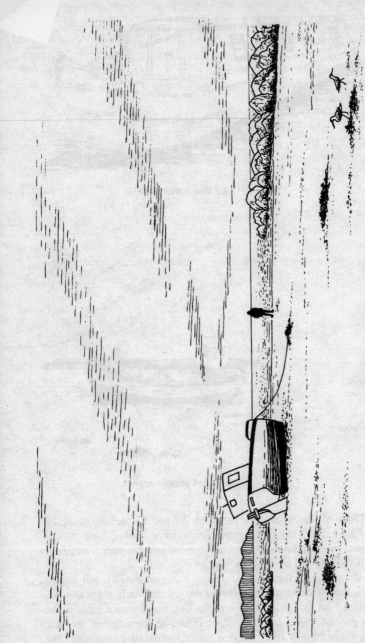

Fig. 57 Natural mini-harbours.

boat is not slap bang in the middle of the picture. As you will discover in the next chapter, placing it dead-centre would show bad composition. The object of attention is best put to one side so that the drawing is not divided into two. Simple when you know how, isn't it? Copy this example or a similar one.

Quiz
1. Give one good composition point.
2. Where should the main mast of a sailing boat be?
3. Which lines are best used to depict the sea?
4. How can you draw sun reflecting from rocks?

Answers
1. Encourage your viewer to look into your picture.
2. Towards the bow.
3. Short, wavy ones, sometimes of different thicknesses.
4. By using the white paper to show against any shading.

8
Be A Good Composer

You may now feel confident enough to tackle drawing from photographs. To be successful you also need to know how to compose a good picture. A camera records things as they are rather than as an artist wants them to be. Most of us become snap-happy when we are on holiday. What looks perfectly lovely through a view-finder often turns out tiny and distant in the resulting snapshot. Somehow it can seem only half the scene you expected. Photographs can nevertheless provide excellent information for a drawing.

As an artist you are free to alter any scene you choose to draw. Two of the greatest English painters changed what they saw in order to produce great works of art. They were John Constable and JW Turner. I recall visiting a waterfall in the Yorkshire Dales, specially to see where one magnificent masterpiece had been painted. The painting concerned was done with sparkling golds, yellows and the brilliant use of white and colour to create hazy water-splash and mist. What I found when I got to the force (waterfall) was a let down. The water trickled over a black rock ledge, only to splash down onto more dark rocks. Perhaps the weather had been too dry for too long – but then, I cannot claim Turner's vision or superb technique.

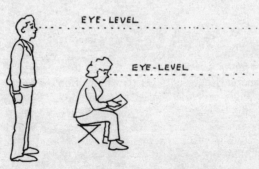

Fig. 58 Different eye-levels.

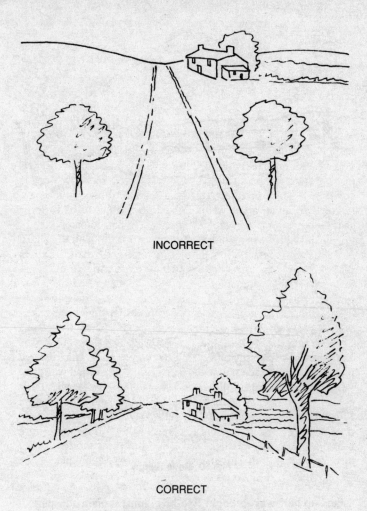

INCORRECT

CORRECT

Fig. 59 The eye-level is important.

Common faults

Beginner artists tend to ignore composition both through lack of knowledge and the struggle to put down accurate lines. Composition in art refers to the arrangement of things. The most common mistake is to put the horizon far too high up in a drawing. Eye-level in any picture must fall on the imaginary line which lies directly ahead of you when you draw that scene. See figure 58. You cannot start drawing a landscape seated and

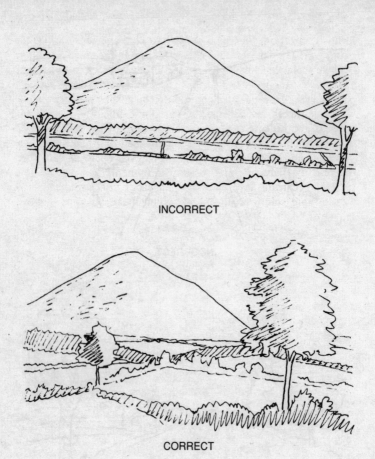

INCORRECT

CORRECT

Fig. 60 Move things.

stand up half-way through! Eye-level must remain constant.

A low horizon will give an impression of great space and calm. You can easily test how different eye-levels affect pictures. Look at whatever scene is in front of you now. Stand on a chair or bench to look; then sit down and, finally, lie down to look. The latter position is one sometimes used by photographers and artists to give an unusual view point. For most purposes, however, the ideal level for the horizon is about one third of the way up from the bottom edge of a drawing.

Figure 59 illustrates correct and incorrect eye-levels. It also shows another aspect of composition. The two trees in the top

70

drawing are both the same shape and size and are equidistant from you. They therefore divide attention. In the correct version I have balanced one tree against three, placed at different distances. You now see the house as the object of attention.

The next example of a common error is shown in figure 60. The top sketch has a series of horizontal lines, two opposing trees, and a hill in the centre. The lower drawing demonstrates improvements that you can make. Shift the hill off centre, move the trees and rearrange the fields so that the eye is led into the scene. Buy shares in earth-moving equipment!

When learning how to draw landscapes you are tempted to concentrate solely on the items which make up your picture,

INCORRECT

CORRECT

Fig. 61 Keep objects in the scene.

71

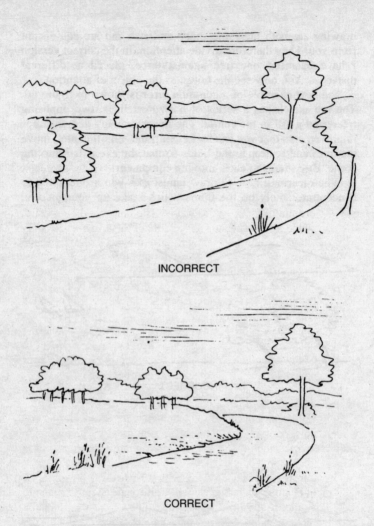

INCORRECT

CORRECT

Fig. 62 Stop a river running out of the scene.

and to forget about composition. Don't worry! You're in the good company of all who started the same way. Figure 61 shows what I mean. The incorrect sketch has two hills, two trees and two boats which appear to be heading out of the scene. The high horizon does not help this faulty composition. Curiously, odd numbers, 1, 3, 5, etc., are an aid to composition. Now study the correct drawing in figure 61. Three boats sail into the picture. Two different size trees are balanced by a broken, rugged shore-line. A lower horizon flattens down the hills, and a distant headland has been added. Just a little thought given before beginning a drawing can make a huge difference to the finished job.

The faulty composition in figure 62 doesn't seem too bad at first glance but look how much better the correct version is. A raised river bank now prevents the river running out of the picture. A large tree on the right balances the small groups on the left. Eye-level has been brought down to give a greater impression of distance.

Figure 63 is very similar in faults to figure 62. The man and his dog are moving out of the frame. The lane is running off at the edge. One tree dominates the middle of the scene whilst only half of another tree tries to get into the act. The re-drawn example has a winding lane. Its previously uniform fence is now broken down and more interesting. Opposite this fence is now a straggly hedge to add balance. The figures move into the set. The trees have been rearranged and the horizon has been brought down slightly.

You can now see how to compose a good landscape picture from almost any holiday snap or from life. Develop the habit of thinking how *you* want others to see your gem. Make your drawings easy to look at – that's good composition!

Use your freedom

Be uninhibited about changing what you see into what you want to portray. Feel free to chop out, pop in, shift, curve, bend, straighten or whatever. Remember, you are an artist not a camera.

There are exceptions to taking such liberties. For example, you might be commissioned by your millionaire aunt or uncle to draw the ancestral home accurately. Then you would show every cracked window-pane, broken roof tile, dent in the ramparts, and patch of rising damp – or would you?

You can glean a great deal about excellence in composition by visiting a good art gallery and studying the work of old masters. The trick, once you have absorbed what you will – having stood in front of a particular masterpiece – is to remember what your eye *first saw* and then, how you looked around the rest of the painting. Next, have a good think. What had the artist done to make your eye move the way it did? What you discover will give you ideas for your own creations.

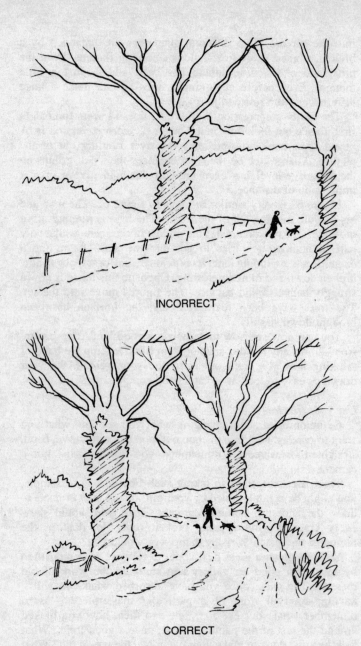

INCORRECT

CORRECT

Fig. 63 Balance trees.

A bad composition is one at which people won't waste time looking. Perhaps it is too confusing to the eye; maybe no single item grabs the attention; possibly there are too many conflicting objects.

Quiz
1. What is good composition?
2. Give four composition faults.
3. Why is your eye-level important?
4. What should figures in a landscape be doing?

Answers
1. An arrangement that is easy to look at.
2. Horizon too high. Picture divided. No balance. Figures or such things as rivers or lanes moving out of the scene.
3. Your eye-level should determine where your horizon is.
4. They should be moving into the picture, or be an integral part of the design.

9
A Useful Little Aid

A grid is a handy little aid for artists of all abilities. It is easy to make one out of a transparent sheet, marked in squares and sandwiched between two cardboard frames. See figure 65.

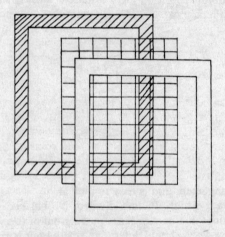

Fig. 65 A grid.

Many famous people in the world of art have used grids. Vincent Van Gogh, for instance, made quite a large one on a stand. He mentioned the gadget in letters to his long-suffering brother who sponsored him throughout his life. Van Gogh used a grid to make a painting of his bed in the asylum at Arles. This picture, which was sold for millions of pounds, is a good example of accurate perspective drawing. Vincent, like me, was a self-taught artist. The comparison ends there – I've no intention of lopping off an ear or shooting myself!

Long before Van Gogh was born artists made grids and used them to study perspective. This artists' tool has been around for a very long time.

How to make a grid

The grid I use was made in half-an-hour from two pieces of scrap cardboard, a sheet of transparent material of the kind used for overhead projectors, and a little glue. The screen is divided into 2cm squares, eight up and the same number across. You can use different measurements or sizes to suit yourself.

Your first job is to mark out squares, in ink, on the transparent sheet. Use a rule or straight edge, and a sharp blade to cut out two identical cardboard frames. These frames should have their external measurements slightly larger than the grid and their internal ones somewhat smaller than the grid. Lay one frame down on a flat surface and put a few dabs of glue along the borders. Carefully position the transparent sheet down onto the cardboard. Prepare the other frame with glue and then lower it down onto the grid so that the two frames stick together. A heavy book on top will hold everything in place until the glue dries. That's all there is to making a very useful drawing aid!

How to use a grid

A grid can be used inside or outside on most subjects. I hold mine at arms' length in my left hand so that, while I am taking frequent squints through it at the object in view, my right hand is free to draw. You can, for example, hold your grid half way to your face in order to view a larger scene. This works well but you must remember for any particular picture always to hold it at the same distance from your eyes and to line it up exactly on the same place each time. For example, on a building, it's best to line up with the corner of a wall or some similar item that you can fairly assume the builder built vertical! Then you can see at once at what angle to draw, say, the gutter line in relation to the horizontal in your picture. Figure 66 will show you what I mean. A grid also helps you draw the right slope on a roof.

From my simple example above you should be able to appreciate how you will also now be able to use a grid to capture accuracy in lines of perspective to a degree you may never have imagined possible before. The same tool can be used in a slightly modified way as an aid to drawing still-life subjects, trees, hills, humans, and no end of other things. First pencil lightly onto your paper or pad the *same number* of squares you have on your grid. You can then make accurate sketches simply by matching what you draw onto your pad squares to what you see in your grid squares.

A grid can also be used to scale a portrait up or down.

Provided the number of squares in the grid you place over a portrait is the *same* as the number of squares on your pad it doesn't matter whether those on your pad are larger or smaller; the point is that if, say, the nose, occupies $2^1/_2$ squares on the portrait grid, then it must fill the same $2^1/_2$ squares on your pad grid. If you keep everything in its rightful square then, be it bigger or smaller your copy will be a true one. If you wanted to you could enlarge the drawings in this book using a grid.

A grid is particularly useful when drawing village scenes from life. A glance through the screen will reveal exactly where the lines of the buildings converge, as their distance from you increases (perspective). You can use it to see just how the edges of a road merge, perhaps round a curve and out of sight, into the distance. It may help you to suggest the camber of a road accurately.

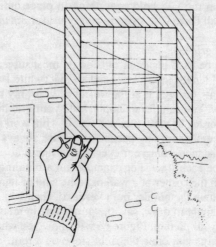

Fig. 66 A useful aid for drawing buildings.

Help with landscapes

Looking through a grid will help you decide what to leave in or take out of a landscape. In other words, how to improve your composition. Study figure 67.

Beginner artists faced with a vast spectacular panorama which covers scores of miles often try to cram the lot onto a small A5 sketch pad! This is a common mistake which use of a grid will prevent. The picture to be drawn in my figure 67, for example, is that part in the frame.

78

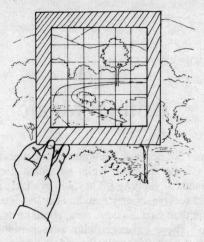

Fig. 67 A grid helps with composition.

If you want to draw a wide landscape, and there's no reason
why you shouldn't, you could still use a grid, but it would have
to be wide enough to cover the scene. This entails making a
much bigger screen. I personally don't think it's worth carting
around more than one small grid. Frequent use of this will teach
you quickly what to look for, and what to draw. You will gain
the experience to tackle panoramic scenes with suitably huge
confidence and enthusiasm without the need for a giant grid.

Quiz
1. Why use a grid?
2. How does a grid help you?
3. What is a grid useful for?

Answers
1. It will improve your drawing.
2. It enables you to get things in their rightful place.
3. You name it!

79

10
Animal Magic

The simple but accurate drawings of the world's first animal artists are still on the cave walls on which they were drawn many thousands of years ago. They will probably remain as long as our planet survives. Early man had far less intelligence and a smaller brain than ours, so how, then, could he draw the animals around him? Those cavemen who were perhaps instinctively artistic had the ability to make good observations. It was important to them to be able to show others of their tribe what sort of animals were available for food.

Looking properly is vital to all drawing. I do not think that early man was gifted. Drawing is a skill rather than a gift although all professions produce the occasional genius. Early man knew how to *look* – the secret of being able to draw!

Cavemen drew with charcoal (burnt wood), coloured clay, earth, and lamp black from their hollowed-out stone lamps. The home-made paint or ink was applied with hands, fingers or a stick. Think of all the advantages you start with!

In order to teach myself how to draw animals I spent many hours observing and sketching in zoos, wildlife parks and natural history museums. You can learn my skills without doing this. Most of the creatures used as examples in this book are common to town and countryside.

Be an Ice Age artist

Ice age artists left behind many examples of their work, some of which was very advanced. The bison was one of their most popular subjects. They hunted this beast for food. It was often drawn in black paint. A few excellent clay models of this animal have also been discovered. Figure 69 shows an Ice Age type drawing of a bison. I have drawn this in easy stages. The top illustration is of the general basic shape. The one below shows how a few details have been added, with the final sketch at the bottom of the page. Notice how few lines there seem to be. I want you to copy this illustration.

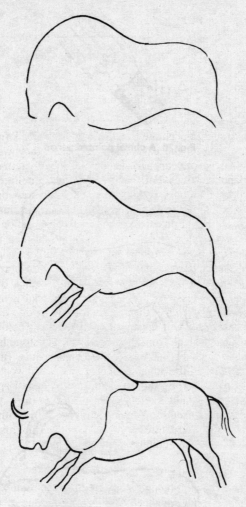

Fig. 69 Try cave art drawing.

First, sharpen your 2B pencil into a chisel point. This is done with a sharp blade rather than a pencil sharpener. The lead should be made into a wedge shape so that it has a wide edge and also a thin side when turned – a chisel point. This is very useful because you have a dual purpose pencil which will give a broad or thin line. See figure 70.

81

Fig. 70 A chisel pointed pencil.

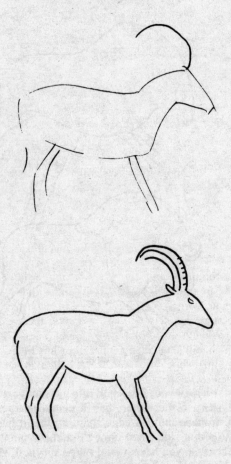

Fig. 71 Draw an ibex.

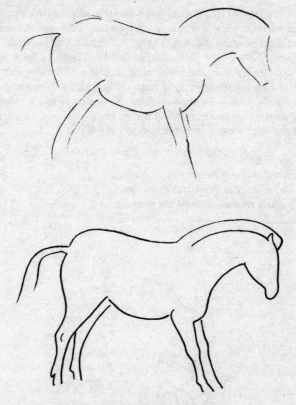

Fig. 72 Sketch this Ice Age horse.

Now continue your work by taking a long look at the examples in figures 71 and 72. Then, with the same pencil, lightly put down the essential lines of each as you tackle it. When you are happy with these, ink over them using your size 0.1 pen. When it is dry (about one minute) erase only the pencil lines which still show, and admire your handiwork!

The animal shown in figure 71 is called an ibex. It's a goat-like creature which inhabits remote mountainous regions in Europe. The ibex was once very plentiful but is now only found in small numbers. Take a look at the overall shape of the animal. Then try to sketch it quickly and boldly. Remember that once you get the basic shape right you will have a correct structure to work on. Adding the detail of the eye and horn markings will then be quite easy.

In France and Spain there are some remarkable cave drawings of prehistoric horses. These stocky animals had stiff manes and short legs. Figure 72 will show you how to draw your own versions. Notice how the use of so few bold lines by early artists did not detract from the power and accuracy of their work.

Ice Age artists portrayed many other kinds of animal. The mammoth, which we tend to think of as a huge hairy elephant, was smaller than our jumbo of today. Foxes, wolves, bears, lions and reindeer were immortalized on cave walls.

Points to note
1. You can draw better than cavemen.
2. Be bold, confident and enthusiastic.
3. Expect mistakes, they are normal.

11
Count Sheep

You can now move from the Ice Age to the present day for the remainder of this book. I am going to show you how easy it will be for you to draw sheep. You may have noticed, when out of town, how many sheep there are. Thousands and thousands of them graze in meadows, fields, up mountains, almost everywhere. They are all pretty much alike in body shape – only their faces differ. There are white-faced sheep such as the Cheviot, Welsh Mountain, Southdown and Romney breeds, while species of black-faced sheep include the Suffolk, Blackface, Yorkshire and Shropshire varieties.

Oblong with rounded ends

The basic shape of a sheep reminds me of an oblong with rounded ends, added to which are a thin leg at each corner, and a small wedge-shaped head. Once you get this image fixed in your mind you will *always* know how to set about drawing the animal.

The *detailed* shape of an animal can be suggested by the way fur, hair or markings are drawn. The body and limbs are rounded, like our own bits and pieces, so it would be wrong to use straight lines to depict hair or fur. Beginners tend to do just this, and then wonder why their animal appears to be flat sided. It is a help to pencil in lightly half-ovals as a guide. Figure 74 illustrates what I mean.

Pay particular attention to the way I have drawn the wool coat. This was done with small wavy dashes running over the body contours and also down or along the outline of the coat – just the way it grows on the real creature. A few tiny dots on the face and legs denote skin texture. You should find figure 74 quite easy to copy.

Remember to *construct* every one of your drawings from a basic complete outline inwards. This is vital in all work. Many artists try to draw what they see a line at a time, in isolation from the whole. This is a big mistake because one wrong line –

perhaps too long or too short – will cause all lines that follow to be wrong. Avoid this trap.

Animals, like people, do not stay still in one position just to please artists. For example, sheep will look round at you. As it happens this is a good pose. See figure 75 of a Suffolk ewe.

Study the construction lines which fit into an imaginary box. Note how I have suggested ridges of thick wool. It isn't necessary to cover the whole animal with these markings. Indeed, doing that could make the drawing rather boring. All sheep have cleft hooves. Copy this example using my methods. I'm sure that you will achieve a super likeness and raise your own game as a budding artist within a matter of a few moments.

Fig. 74 Oblong with rounded ends.

Fig. 75 Draw a Suffolk ewe.

You must have noticed that sheep spend most of their waking time eating. I have heard them chomping away during the middle of the night. Figure 76 was drawn to show you how they look when feeding their little faces. Notice how the body curves have been suggested. When seen from a distance the eyes of a black-faced sheep are not visible. Grass is suggested by short criss-cross strokes. Copy these examples.

Lamb without mint sauce

Young animals have great appeal for most folk. Lambs, you will be pleased to learn, are far easier to draw than children! Little lambs have long legs, undeveloped coats and rounded heads. It is amazing how a beautiful little lamb quickly grows into a cumbersome over-weight adult. (After mature sheep are

87

sheared they become, once more, leggy animals.) See how the rounded bodies of little lambs are suggested in figure 77. Draw your own versions of these.

Get close

A good animal portrait makes an attractive picture. I have chosen the handsome ram's head used as an emblem by Yorkshire National Park for the sketch in figure 79. It is not wise to approach a ram closely. It might take exception to having you on its territory. They are very powerful animals. I was once charged by a young ram but escaped injury by leaping onto the

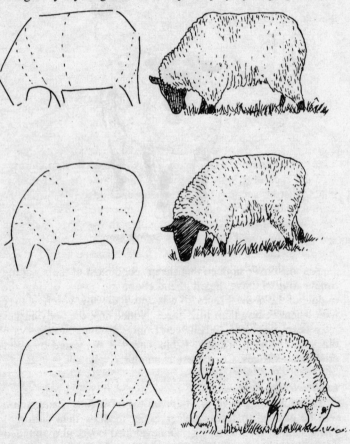

Fig. 76 Draw sheep feeding.

Fig. 77 Lambs are leggy.

top of a large bale of straw! Take no chances: observe them, as I do, from behind a wall, fence, hedge or in a cattle market.

Take a careful look at figure 78. See how the construction lines must be accurate before details are added. Your problem here is to draw the horns correctly. In many rams the two horns do not match each other. My example shows this. Sketch, in pencil, the wedge-shaped face before putting in the curly horns. Start as in the top illustration in figure 78. Then add the outlines of where the dark patches are to go. See the lower illustration. Pencil in the nostrils, mouth and eye.

Now go to figure 79 to see how all the shading is done. The optical illusion of round horn is obtained by using curved lines to suggest the form. Put in a few battle scars over and around the curved lines. The dark patches of hair are best created by making scores of tiny lines which follow the direction they grow on the animal. You will need to look carefully in order to get this right. Pop in a few lines in the white areas. Draw the long body hair as straggly streamers which point downwards. Sketch in the eye. Cast a critical look over your drawing then start to ink it in. This advanced picture will take a little time. I feel sure that you will manage it. Make space on your sideboard for your little gem!

Go for it

I once came across a group of pretty creatures called Jacob's sheep. These are an ancient breed which are now gaining popularity. The lambs had black blotches against pure white. The adults had patches of dark brown. I sketched the original for figure 80 after watching them for half an hour.

I want you to copy this scene by working out for yourself the different basic shapes of the animals. Once you have done this correctly, in pencil, the drawing is quite straightforward. Pay particular attention to the curved back of one lamb, the stocky legs, shoulder blades, and rounded head. The standing lamb is

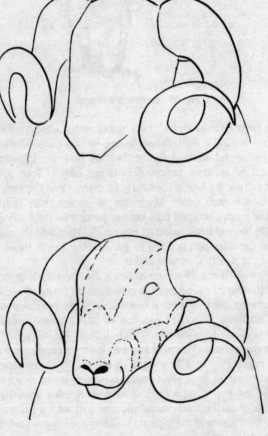

Fig. 78 The first construction lines.

Fig. 79 The finished ram drawing.

Fig. 80 Draw these Jacob's sheep.

nibbling the ear of its twin. Mother, in the background, keeps her eye on them. You will use lots of dots and dashes as shown in my drawing. When your pencil sketch is complete draw over it with a size 0.1 pen. This is an ambitious picture but there is nothing in it which you can't do. Your finished masterpiece could make a nice greetings card for your spouse, friend or bank manager! Go for it!

Assignments
1. In ink or pencil draw any animal from a photograph.
2. Choose an animal from this chapter. Look at it for three minutes. Close the book then quickly draw it. Check your result.
3. Try the same system working from a live animal. It could be a pet dog, cat or a sheep.

12
Be Up To Scratch With Cats

This chapter is devoted to teaching you how to draw the type of cat found in every village, town and city in this country: the short-haired domestic moggie which is also popular the world over. If you can sketch a cat accurately then you will be able to draw any creature. It is the pet most frequently drawn by beginner artists. We shall spend extra time learning how to depict this fascinating animal.

Cats of all kinds are my favourite animal subjects. I like to watch them, stroke them, talk to them, draw, paint and sculpt them. The graceful way they move gives an impression of hidden power. A flexible coat and spine allows them to adopt a wide range of interesting poses.

The hardest problem solved

When you can correctly draw a cat's face you have solved the hardest part of the job. Many people go wrong here because a cat's skull structure is not easy to fathom at first glance. The bone formation is hidden by muscle and fur. If your first cat picture resembles a lop-sided plum pudding with eyes and ears, don't worry – you are about to bring your cats up to scratch!

Unlike dogs, all cats have a similar face. Once you can draw cats you should be capable of portraying their big relations, tigers, lions, leopards and right through the 37 species of the feline family.

Like millions of other people I have a pet cat. She adopted me when she was a five month old stray kitten. She knew a mug when she saw one! It is likely that our domestic cat is descended from ancestors who lived in ancient Egypt 4,000 years ago. Cats were then deemed to be gods and treated as such. My own pet seems aware of this, judging by the way she demands instant attention and easily manipulates me into obtaining exactly what she wants.

I have reminded her that in Medieval days the Church, quite wickedly, pronounced all cats to be devils. My moggie dismissed this bit of history with an imperious look and angry twitch of her tail. She probably knew that, as a result of one silly Pope's decree, cats were cruelly persecuted for years; this happened despite cats being worth their weight in gold during the Great Plague, which was caused by millions of rats. I call my pet, TC (Top Cat). We shall use her as a model for many of the exercises that follow.

Figure 82 shows some quick sketches of TC. Examine the two profiles. The 3-dimensional feel is achieved by adding fur sparingly, first put in with dotted lines.

See the way the ears have been drawn. A cat's ear has a thick ridge round the base at the rear, as shown in the lower illustration.

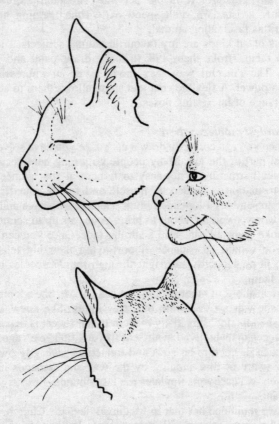

Fig. 82 A close-up of a cat's head.

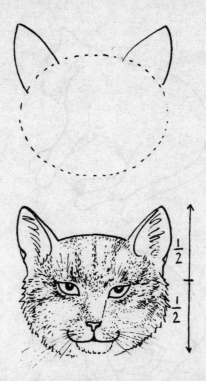

Fig. 83 How to get proportions correct.

Observe how small and delicate the nose is and how cats always seem to be smiling due to a gently curved mouth line. The lower jaw fits snugly into the top jaw.

Most cats have white whiskers but you can depict these with fine black lines. There are a group of six whiskers over each eye, and four or five rows on each side of the mouth. You don't want to put all of them in, just a few will be enough.

My cat has a pronounced forehead. This feature varies slightly from cat to cat, as does the length of the nose. In this respect animal faces are like human faces. Every one is unique to its owner. TC has a short nose. She was dozing when I first sketched her, so her eyes were closed. In my second profile you can see TC doesn't miss a trick when her eyes are open! Cats, by the way, spend three quarters of their lives asleep or resting. This is good for artists!

To begin with, leave out detailed fur. I return to help you with that shortly. Remember, you will also help yourself by making all

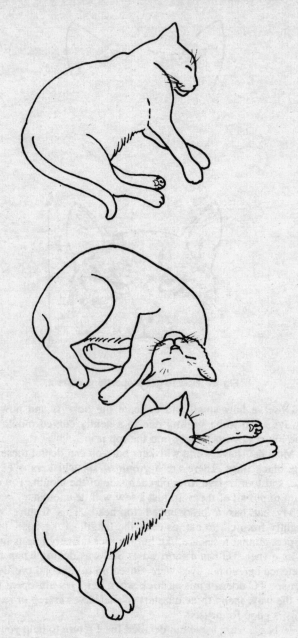

Fig. 84 Sleeping positions.

your drawings larger than the printed versions can be in this book. Copy figure 82 carefully. It is a key to drawing all cats well.

Drawing a cat's face from the front should not give you any more trouble than a profile sketch – once you learn where each feature should go. The most common errors I see beginners make include drawing the cat's nose too big and the ears perfectly triangular, which they are not. In fact they are petal-like in structure with curved ends. There is a small kink at the base of the outer rim. Newcomers to art tend to draw the eyes too large and too high in the face. There is black skin round a cat's eyes. We normally see the bottom half of this. The top half is usually covered by a fold of skin – a cat's eyelid. However, in a drawing, little more than the outline shape of the eye is enough to portray it without excess detail intruding.

Study figure 83. Notice that the basic shape is oval. The ears are elliptical. Roughly half way between ear tips and bottom of the lower jaw is where the eyes look out. Half way between the eyebrows and lower jaw line is where the *top* of the nose is. With a little practice you will soon automatically get these proportions right. Copy this example in pencil; then ink it in. Practise drawing some more cat heads from life, from books or from your photo album until you can do them from memory. This will be a big advance for you.

Fig. 85 Dots and dashes depict coat markings.

Let sleeping cats lie
When you can draw a sleeping cat accurately you will then be able to draw one in any position. A sleeping moggie may be deep in dreamland and appear to be motionless, but no sooner

Fig. 86 A watching cat.

do you start sketching than it will suddenly twitch, stretch, and assume a different position! A cat resting, however, will normally remain in the same pose for a long time.

The secret is to observe carefully and then quickly jot down the basic shape. After that it doesn't matter if the cat moves because you can take your time adding the little details.

Figure 84 shows my cat TC in three sleeping positions. See how her legs and head have been drawn. Draw figure 84 twice the size of the printed examples. Use pen or pencil.

Put coat markings in last. Remember how to convey the curve of body, muscle and limb, by the way you make your marks on the paper. TC is a multi-coloured tortoiseshell cat. Figure 85 will show you how I have depicted her fur markings. It is the same technique that was used for the ram's head illustration in Chapter 11. Study the way I have used fine lines, dots and dashes to give an illusion of different colours and tones. With most modern drawing pens you can work very fast. The ink will not smudge easily. You can produce an excellent pencil drawing by using a hard pencil (H) for the outline then a soft one (4B) to give middle tones and deep shades. Beautiful pencil drawings are quite rare. Don't ignore this medium which, in fact, is easier than pen work. Copy figure 85. In this pose she was sitting on her tail which can just be seen poking between her hind legs. If your drawing goes wrong, don't worry. Look again and then re-draw. It pays to be determined and patient.

Fig. 87 Draw a tabby cat.

Watch it watching

As mentioned previously, a cat spends much of its time resting. My pet, for example, will stay in a comfortable position for ages if she is watching her territory from the vantage point of a window-sill inside the kitchen. Figure 86 gives the rounded basic shapes which combine to make up the outline drawing. The lower illustration shows TC when she looks round to see what I'm up to. Copy these sketches in pencil or pen. Fill in the fur details in the top illustration.

Fig. 88 Wash and brush-up poses.

A friend's pet was used as a model for figure 87. She is a large tabby with a nice gentle disposition. The markings on her coat were created in the same manner as for figure 85. She has very dark markings along her back, her stripes are black and her face and chest are white. Draw your version of this tabby cat. Although you are copying my work your efforts will not be exactly like mine. This is good because you are developing your own unique style. You could become the best cat artist in the world!

Clean cats

Cats spend a good deal of their time grooming. They are one of the cleanest animals around. They always follow the same procedure when having a wash and brush up: they begin with their paws; then comes the head, followed by flanks, body and the tail last of all. During their ablutions they make many interesting shapes. Figure 88 shows you some grooming positions. Draw a page or two of these, and have a shot at putting in the markings as I have done in the top sketch. Make your studies larger than mine.

Fig. 89 Draw a little tiger.

Moving moggies

Moggies on the move are graceful creatures. At times they go like lightning, much too fast for our eyes to see. Figure 89 was drawn from a quick sketch made when I saw a visiting little tiger in my garden. See, as *always*, how the basic shape was first jotted down before finishing the drawing. The stripes were put in with a size 0.5 pen. All the tiny dots are drawn with a 0.1 pen.

My moggie seems to hate others of her kind though she likes people. She will normally attack any moggie who enters her territory. The battle is usually short and sharp. Fur flies everywhere but it isn't hers! I once watched her as she confronted a dog fox who trotted down the garden path. She

Fig. 90 Draw an angry cat.

102

Fig. 91 Draw this kitten.

transformed herself by puffing out her fur. Her tail closely resembled that of the fox. She hissed loudly. The fox cautiously walked round her then went on its way. Figure 90 is my impression of an angry cat. See how you get on with this one.

Kittens are popular

Kittens, like all baby animals, have a lot of appeal and are very popular subjects with the buying public. Kittens seem to have huge ears. This is because they grow slower from birth than the rest of the head and it seems to be nature's way for them to start proportionally larger. Have a look at the kitten in figure 91. Build a basic shape from this, then make a finished drawing. It should be good enough to make a little present for your favourite cat person. Tackle the portrait of the long-haired kitten in figure 92 next. Notice the large eyes and ears. The long fur is best drawn with quick, loose strokes. Try it.

Fig. 92 A long-haired kitten.

Assignments
1. From life or photographs draw three different cat heads.
2. Do the same with complete cats.
3. Watch a cat for a while. Then look down at your drawing pad and capture the outline shape with deft strokes. Check your effort by looking at your subject again. Now tackle detail such as face, tail and claws. You can sneak another look whenever necessary. Finally, draw the fur markings.

13
Be Foxy

I live in a large city yet the wild animal I most frequently see is the fox. This elegant, intelligent creature has been around man since the Stone Age. Thousands of years ago it learned that where man was there were likely to be free meals available. Today, as never before, the wily fox has established itself in every town and city. In an urban environment it is safe from the hunt, but victim of motorists. Many are killed on our roads.

Shortly after I took up residence in my house three fox cubs and their parents began to use my garden as a short cut to their earth which was under a tumbledown shed next door. Beyond the end of my patch there are neglected gardens which are covered in brambles and sprouting ash trees. It is a paradise for foxes. I have been able to study and sketch them almost daily.

Draw a portrait of Reynard

The fox got the name of Reynard many hundreds of years ago. The name means "unconquerable through his cleverness". It is a very apt title for this resourceful animal which has an ultra-sensitive sense of smell, keen hearing and excellent vision. Farmers hate it on account of their livestock, countrymen hunt it with hounds, but millions of ordinary folk admire it. It is a pleasant sight in our city gardens.

The hardest problem you have in drawing a fox is getting the head to look right. This, of course, is true of sketching most animals. I have included figure 94 to show how to draw a profile of a fox. Notice the large elliptical ears which have a small kink in the outer rim – similar to that of a cat. The fox has a long pointed snout, large nose, and flared cheeks of white hair. The mask-like face is made more distinctive by dark tear-like marks from the corners of the eyes. This animal is a member of the dog family, but it is like a cat in the way it is agile. Copy figure 94 in pencil.

Figure 95 is what you see when a fox looks at you. City bred cubs and vixens (females) do not seem to have a fear of man like

Fig. 94 A fox in profile.

Fig. 95 A fox looking at you.

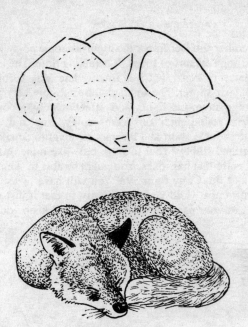

Fig. 96 A still fox to draw.

that of a country fox. Those that live in my neck-of-the-woods will let me approach quite near before moving off.

A frontal view clearly shows the marvellous white fringe round the face. Copy this example in pen or pencil.

Easy poses

On most sunny Spring and Summer mornings I can look out of a bedroom window and see a fox or two basking on a shed roof. They like the sun and will curl up for long spells to sleep in its warmth. Sometimes I have crept slowly and quietly down the garden to get a close up sketch of a sleeping fox but the fox has a sixth sense. The closed eyes suddenly spring open; it becomes fully alert and ready to disappear quickly. Despite foxes being so common in towns many people never see one. I think this is because they don't expect to see one, and don't look for it. I hope that you will now search your area for Reynard.

Look at figure 96 to see how the basic outline of a sleeping fox is turned into a finished sketch. Lots of dots and dashes again feature. Copy this and then turn to figure 97. This is the view I often get when fox watching. Draw your own version.

107

Chubby cubs

In November and December the nights become noisy with the blood-curdling screams of foxes. It is mating time. The cubs are born in March or April, but it is usually late May before I see the current year's litter. The small chubby cubs are very playful. They indulge in mock fights and affectionately groom each other. When young their fur seems spiky, fine and dark in colour. The snout is short and the ears have yet to develop. The tail is short and stubby. Your town or city, like mine, may have a Nature Centre that has foxes. You might be able to sketch them from life as I do. Copy figure 98. You will have to use lots of dots to draw cubs. Hold your pen lightly so that it just touches the surface of your paper. It takes time but will keep you off the streets!

Fig. 97 A fox is quickly alert.

Fig. 98 Chubby fox cubs.

Hunter and scrounger

The fox is highly intelligent and is a great survivor. Its wonderful nose can soon pinpoint a food supply whether it is a fat fieldmouse, a bird, or a turkey carcass in a dustbin. During the worst of winter, foxes can be seen tipping bins over to rake out anything edible. At dawn I have watched a dog fox nip under the gate of a Primary School, cross a playground, and inspect a row of bins. Litter louts who leave a trail of chips, fish remains, curry and other food about the streets provide the fox with supper. Foxes eat vegetables as well as meat.

I sketched a vixen eating cat food which my over-fussy moggy had left. After she had eaten she turned the dish over. From then on, I always knew when she had been around. Figure 99 is my impression of her feeding. Sketch the basic outline, then draw her.

109

I don't regularly feed the foxes because they quickly take advantage of the situation. After putting out free meals for them a family of foxes began to visit my garden frequently. They dug huge holes everywhere. The vixen would sit and stare through the kitchen window. It was very interesting, but I had also to consider the safety of my pet cat, TC. While she is young she can take care of herself, but there is evidence that cats that are old, weak or injured are eaten by foxes. I have noted that stray cats tend to disappear when there are growing fox cubs about. Have a look at my drawing of a fox hunting in my garden, figure 100. Copy this. By now you should be quite good, if not brilliant, at animal drawing. It will help you to look back at your early efforts to see how you have improved.

Fig. 99 A vixen eating cat food.

Fig. 100 Draw a fox hunting.

Assignments
1. Choose two illustrations from this chapter, then look at them for one minute. Close the book and draw them from memory after first drawing a basic outline.
2. Draw foxes from photographs.
3. Go out and draw foxes from life – or through a bedroom window!

14
Bright-Eyed And Bushy-Tailed

The grey squirrel, like the fox, is another wild animal which has taken to our towns in a big way. It is an intelligent, attractive creature which is also a great pest. Despite man it is a resourceful survivor found in many of our parks, woods and cities.

The grey squirrel was introduced a few hundred years ago from North America. It quickly spread throughout the country and was thought to have displaced the native red squirrel. Today this theory is no longer acknowledged by experts. They now think that the red squirrel has become rare because its habitat has shrunk, which is a much more likely explanation.

Just round the corner from where I live there is a busy main road which is lined by tall trees. Grey squirrels build their nests, or drays, in these on a level with the bus's upper deck passengers! If folk are observant they can watch them while on their way to work.

Draw cheeky chops

The grey squirrel quickly learns who it can trust and of whom it can take advantage. Children feed it in parks and gardens.

Grey squirrels frequently pay a visit to my garden to raid the bird food or dig up newly planted flower bulbs. My cat used to chase them into a nearby rowan tree. For a long time the squirrels could always out-climb the cat, but one day she managed to corner a young squirrel in my neighbour's porch. I thought that she would kill the youngster but all she wanted to do was sniff noses with it. From then on the mad pursuits stopped.

You will find that the head shape of a squirrel, which is a rodent, is very similar to that of a mouse or rabbit. You can see this by looking at figure 102. See also the way I have suggested the tail by drawing longish pen strokes which generally radiate around the tail itself. The fur nearest the tail bone is dark grey but this turns to white at the outside. To achieve this impression I have left white space in abundance at the back of the tail. I used short lines which go the same way as it grows on the

Fig. 102 Draw a grey squirrel.

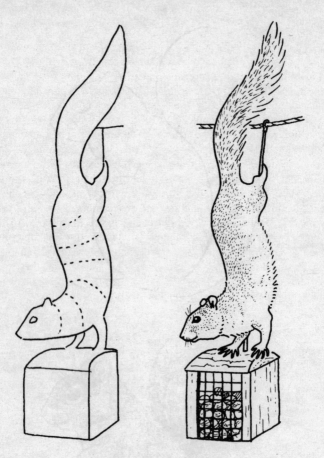

Fig. 103 A hungry squirrel.

animal to suggest body fur texture. You will notice that the squirrel has small rounded ears, short whiskers, dark eyes outlined by white or cream fur, long hind legs and toes, and human-like hands. Copy the basic outline first and then draw meticulously in pencil or pen. You might try drawing the tree branch. See how the roundness of this has been suggested by short curved pen strokes. Isn't it easy when you know how?

Always bear in mind when drawing any animal that if you draw the main shape accurately the rest is relatively easy. In other words, *looking* at the overall profile of the pose is more than half the job.

Changing shapes

The grey squirrel, like so many animals, can suddenly change shape dramatically. It is a very agile creature which can climb and bound across open ground at great speed. You may have seen the grey squirrel's intellect featured on television. Scooping up bird food left on a bird table is no problem at all to the enterprising squirrel. However, it is more often filmed, instead, overcoming one obstacle after another in order to get to food. One little fellow who visited my garden showed the same sort of intelligence. I had hung a bag of peanuts on a clothes line. The food was meant to give the birds a bit of help during a cold spell. The squirrel bit through the line then took its time to eat the spilled nuts. This happened twice more. I then put up a wire line. Did I win? No! Figure 103 is my impression of the squirrel concerned. It scampered along the line upside down then slid down the wire supporting the nut cage. It pulled away the grid and tucked in.

Study figure 103 then copy this in pencil or pen. Notice the flowing lines made by tail and body and how the head is angled out.

The rare red squirrel

A few people are lucky enough to have the rare red squirrel as a garden visitor but most of us would have to explore remote regions in order to see this pretty animal. The one time I have

Fig. 104 Draw the rare red squirrel.

Fig. 105 Another view of the red squirrel.

seen it in the wild was on a ramble through a beech wood in the Lake District. The red squirrel is unmistakable. It has a lovely red coat and long tufts of hair on its ears. It is an animal which is found more often in Scotland than in England, where it is confined to small regions of beech wood or coniferous forest. The red squirrel is smaller and slimmer than the chubby grey one. It also has longer fur. The squirrel sketched for figure 104 is in a common pose, sitting up to eat. See how I have drawn the animal and the branch upon which it sits. Copy this example in pencil or pen.

Squirrels are best observed through binoculars while in the shelter of a bush or hide. They are very nervous creatures which move rapidly. They spring from branch to branch before suddenly stopping to listen or look. This is the pose I sketched for figure 105. You can clearly see how the hair radiates from the central bone. This is your next exercise, but scale it up larger than the printed version.

Assignments
1. Study the basic outline in figures 102, 104 and 105. Draw them from memory.
2. Draw a squirrel from a good photograph. Include a bit of the background.
3. Observe and draw grey squirrels from life.

15
Gee Up

Horses are another ever-popular subject for artists and the general public. We shall work on a few of the scores of different kinds of horse. The much used and abused horse was one of the first wild animals to be tamed and domesticated by man. It has been used for a very wide range of jobs: ploughing, pulling heavy loads, carrying knights in armour and transporting whole armies. Without the mighty Shire horse it is doubtful whether, prior to the advent of the internal combustion engine, we could have fed our population growth as we did. Many elderly people still recall seeing these wonderful animals working in the fields and hauling heavy loads through our towns.

Horses have been used by man for centuries for riding, hunting, racing, performing, and so on.

The hardest part first

In my opinion, the most difficult part of a horse to draw is the head because the skull is quite complex. It has many small bumps, hollows, ridges and curves. A head from the side (profile) is wedge shaped. See figure 107. Study the way I have suggested bone under skin by using very fine dot stipple. Horses have big eyes, heavy upper eyelids, with long lashes. Their cheeks are prominent; they have a bony ridge down to the nostrils which are surrounded by soft skin. Copy this illustration then move to figure 108. The head from the front is rather like the shape of a coffin. Try to memorize these shapes because then you will be able to draw a horse head from memory. Copy figure 108.

The whole lot

You may be an accomplished horseman or woman and know far more than I about the anatomy of a horse, in which case you should have few problems in drawing a whole animal. We always draw well the things we know best. This is why artists need to learn how things are put together.

I have had just one riding lesson in my life. A young horse

Fig. 107 Use dot stipple to shade in skin texture.

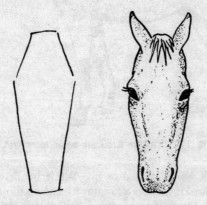

Fig. 108 Coffin-shaped head.

Fig. 109 Draw an accurate basic form first.

called Rocket was allocated to me. While bouncing painfully along I imagined myself as a famous film star galloping through the Valley of Death. Later, after I had dismounted the frisky beast, someone commented that I was an awful rider. There is all too often a spoilsport around. My horse power has a wheel at each corner nowadays!

My sketch of a horse, figure 109, will give you an idea of the general build of the animal. It will also demonstrate how dot stipple is used to show muscle, form and body shape. It is a most useful, yet simple, technique. Draw this example by starting with an accurate basic construction, then add the details. Be sure to position the eye in the correct place, and note how hooves, tail and mane are suggested.

A good big one

My favourite horse is the gentle giant called a Shire. This immensely powerful animal is one of the largest in the world. Its ancestors were the Medieval Great Horses which were bred in the Midland Shires. Hence its name. For all its size and strength it is a friendly, easily managed animal which is making a welcome return to farms, transport concerns and brewers' dreys.

When I was a small schoolboy I once came across a Shire in a field flanked by a dry stone wall. I climbed on top of the wall then struggled onto the broad back of the horse. It didn't seem to mind. We trotted round the field. This exercise was repeated for several days. Then disaster came upon me in the form of an enraged owner who bellowed that the old horse was retired and not up to giving pests like me free rides. We all make little mistakes don't we?

Have a look at figure 110. Observe the sturdy legs, large feet mantled by long hair called feathers, the strong neck, shoulders and massive hind legs. A Shire horse can pull a load of five tonnes with no trouble. Copy this drawing in the usual way.

Wild ponies

The wild ponies on Dartmoor are used to people. Thousands of tourists stop to admire, feed and photograph them. The ponies are small, tough, trustworthy animals who generally like children. The lower drawing in figure 111 is of a Dartmoor pony. Copy this by first drawing out the basic shape.

The upper sketch in figure 111 is my drawing of an Exmoor pony. This is rare compared to the Dartmoor pony. I have seen this animal mixed up with a Red deer herd. In the winter the Exmoor pony grows a thick coat of hair. After walking those moors in January I know that it has the right idea! When summer comes it moults to a thinner coat. What a wise animal. This pony is stronger and sturdier than the Dartmoor species.

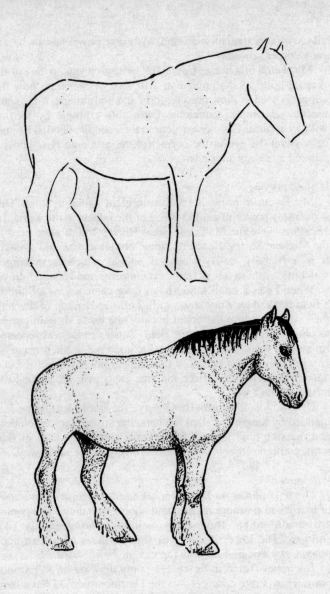

Fig. 110 Draw this Shire horse.

Work out the basic shape for each of these wild ponies; then complete each one in pencil or pen.

Fig. 111 An Exmoor and a Dartmoor pony.

Draw an action horse

It was not until the camera was invented that the action of a running animal became evident to us. When a cine-camera film could freeze the fast-moving legs of a horse, for example, artists and others knew for the first time how to get their drawings right. For centuries artists had tended to sketch and paint running animals with their front legs out and the hind legs stretched back in a similar way. When we look at pictures of Victorian hunt scenes, for instance, we see horse, hound and fox all depicted in this strange position. The movement of animals was, of course, too quick for a human eye to follow, hence the mistake. Three cheers for the camera!

Fig. 112 The action of a horse running.

In actual fact there is a cycle of many different positions for the legs of a horse to be in when it runs. There is one point in a gallop when the animal is balanced on the point of one hoof. I have illustrated just three positions of a galloping horse for figure 112. Study these before copying them. It would help you to draw to a larger scale. Then you could finish off with dot stipple, and perhaps a bit of background, flying turf, and a fleeting shadow.

Fig. 113 Over the sticks.

There is close-up action in my drawing for figure 113. This was drawn from a photograph, using a grid (see Chapter 9). Notice the way movement can be depicted by the horse's flying mane and the way the jockey is crouched forward with one hand on the reins whilst the other clutches a whip. There is a suggestion of a brush fence with bits of it dislodged as the horse jumps over it. Draw your own version of my drawing.

Assignments
1. From a newspaper photograph draw a racehorse. Put in a suggestion of the background.
2. From life or a good picture draw a working Shire horse. Include in your picture a background to depict a farm or similar environment.
3. Draw a wild pony as a possible design for a birthday card. Think about a suitable background and then draw it in.

16

Woof, Woof

Dogs are unique animals. All they seem to want from us is
love, affection, food and shelter. While millions of people keep
dogs there are many owners who do not understand dog
behaviour. Folk do not realise that this popular creature has
strong pack instincts. If the owner is not the pack leader then the
dog will take over this role with sometimes disastrous
consequences. The modern trend towards keeping potentially
lethal guard dogs all too often proves this point. Most household
pets, however, are delightful little chums who are faithful, loyal,
good company and fun.

I have made dogs the last exercise in drawing life-like four-
footed friends in this book because you need to observe so very
accurately before starting to sketch. Unlike domestic cats, dogs
come in all shapes and sizes. All dogs do not share the same
type of skull. Some have deep foreheads while others are
streamlined, stubby, long or whatever. There are so many
different breeds that I can cover only a few of them.

Start with heads

One of my favourite dogs is the Border collie. This wonderful
sheep controller is very popular and has been made more so by
television series which feature sheep dog trials. I once owned a
city-bred collie which was a great pet, but not trained to round
up anything other than me! He was full of energy, very friendly
and good to be with.

Look at my drawings of two adult dogs and a puppy in figure
115. Notice how well defined the foreheads are and the long
snouts. I have left a white line round part of the ears so their
shape can be seen. The black markings, which are quite black on
these animals, were put in with a brush and black drawing ink.
Copy figure 115 by starting with the construction lines, as
shown; then the little details added in become easy. The front
views of heads in figure 116 are slightly more difficult but not
beyond your talent. See how the eyes are drawn between the

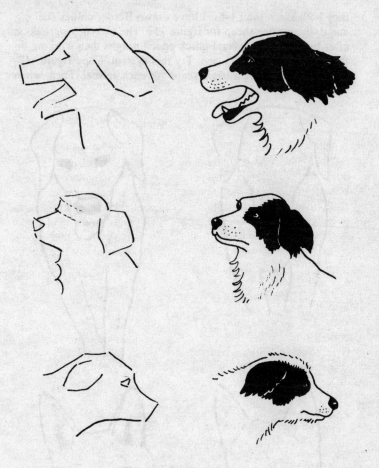

Fig. 115 Profile heads.

dotted lines. If you use pencil for the basic sketch this will help you to produce quickly an accurate illustration. Use dot stipple and tiny lines to depict fur.

A bit of action

Thousands of people are fascinated to watch the way sheep dogs work. The collie, for example, seems to control sheep fully by simply fixing its eyes on them. The sheep immediately look worried but do exactly what the shepherd and the dog want – if

127

they both know their jobs. I have drawn Border collies stalking and dashing after sheep for figure 117. The sketches were done after first drawing several quick pencil roughs then working on the best of them with a pen. Try this system. Copy figure 117. Begin with building a basic shape for each animal. Then, when

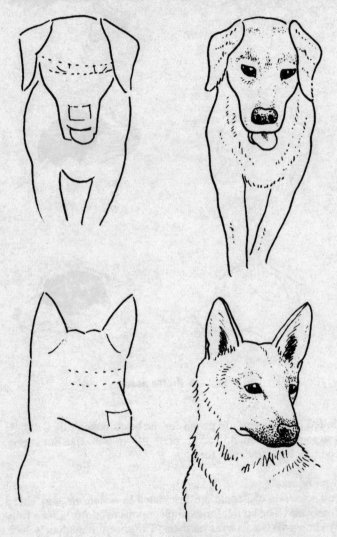

Fig. 116 Draw heads to start you off.

128

Fig. 117 Typical poses.

you are satisfied, finish your gem with your pen.

Another dog seen on television in trials is the Cocker Spaniel, which excels in scenting out and retrieving game birds. Some of these highly skilled animals are worth a small fortune for their

Fig. 118 A Cocker Spaniel.

130

remarkable ability. They are intelligent, obedient creatures who make good pets when not plunging through undergrowth. Study the sketches in figure 118. You will see that I have used a controlled scribble to show the dark brown coat markings. Notice how *much* white I have left showing through. Copy these illustrations in your usual way by starting with a sound basic shape.

Assignments
1. Draw an accurate profile and a front view of your favourite dog.
2. Try to sketch three different breeds of dog. Work from life or photographs.
3. Draw your fast impressions of a dog moving. Use pencil or pen.

17

Feathered Friends

Having worked through this book so far your observation and drawing will be good enough for you to tackle bird art. Depicting our feathered friends requires keen vision, attention to detail, a good memory and ability with pen or pencil. That means you, doesn't it?

Many beginner artists think that birds are much too difficult to sketch because they rarely stay still for long, so they never attempt this fascinating subject. I once thought the same way, but became hooked on identifying the birds around me. I read many books and guides on birds, became increasingly interested in them and then began my art by copying photographs, drawings and specimens in museums. You can begin by copying my ink illustrations. Try using a 2B pencil to make things easier. My complete drawings here in this chapter have close ink shading but you can use very fine pencil lines and then smudge them with your finger to produce a wide range of lovely grey tones.

Heads, beaks and bodies

Bird watching is a very popular hobby for thousands of people. These keen folk are sometimes called "twitchers". A good twitcher can identify a bird in seconds. How is it done? It is a bit like aircraft recognition. The watcher learns about body, head, wing shape, and a lot more, including habitat, colour, flying characteristics, feeding habits, song or call and so on. A would-be bird artist follows the same route – and takes on a new, interesting hobby which can become a nice little earner!

Figure 120 shows the head and beak differences between just four kinds of bird. The top four drawings are of a peregrine falcon. Under this is a duck, then a seagull and at the bottom a member of the finch family. Notice how beak shapes differ. Most artists tend to draw birds in profile because they are easier to identify from this angle. Copy these examples in pencil. Start by drawing the basic shape accurately.

When I want to draw a bird I first take a good look at the

Fig. 120 Different heads and beaks.

overall shape of it. I then jot this down before adding beak, eye, and wing details. It is a construction job. Figure 121 is an example of this. Copy these and try to sketch them quickly. With a little practice you will soon become good enough to draw some birds from memory even after only a fleeting glimpse.

Certain birds which can be seen feeding along sea shores are called waders. One handsome little fellow, a redshank, was the subject for figure 122. Notice how simple these fast impressions have been kept. See how a bird can stretch or contract its neck, and the way it uses its long legs. Try to extend your skill by studying figure 122 for two minutes then jotting down what you saw. This is excellent practice for drawing from life.

Fig. 121 Simply drawn body shapes.

Fig. 122 Fast sketches from life.

Recently, when watching birds on Derwentwater in the Lake District, I saw an angry male swan attack and kill a large duck. The poor duck was grabbed by its neck then held under water until it drowned. Not content with murder the swan swung the corpse round and round for five minutes. Swans are well known for defending their mate, young or nests, but in this case the swan seemed to be totally alone on the lake. These impressive birds all belong to the Queen. Maybe the one I watched will end up in the Tower of London! When swans are on guard they are rather like a battleship cruising into action. I drew one like this for figure 123. I used a fine pen for putting in the feather detail. Always remember to leave a white spot in the upper eye. This keeps the swan awake! Draw your version of this swan.

Fig. 123 Draw this swan.

Little dinosaurs in the garden

Birds are now thought to be the only living relatives of dinosaurs because they have a similar bone structure, are warm-blooded, lay eggs and make nests. Maybe it's just as well that the garden variety is small. Who would fancy daily feeding of huge flying monsters? In this country the most common bird must be the humble sparrow which is a handsome little chap. Figure 124 has one at the top, with a greenfinch in the middle and a chaffinch at the bottom. I have drawn wing and feather details to show you how they fit together, but it's not necessary to put in all these items when producing fast sketches from life. The amount of such detail which you can see decreases with distance. Notice how the three species seem to look alike, but a close study reveals slightly different wing, tail and beak formation. Try drawing these birds twice the size of the printed ones. Start with a correct basic shape and then add in the bits and pieces.

Those of us who have a garden may frequently see a thrush or blackbird searching for a tasty worm or two. These two birds are alike in build but totally different in colouring. While writing this I am able to watch a mother blackbird collect insects

Fig. 124 Common garden birds.

137

for her young which are in a nest close to my window. From time-to-time I rush out into the garden to scare off a marauding cat, magpie and/or the occasional squirrel. All are enemies of young garden birds. Copy the examples in figure 125.

Fig. 125 A thrush and a blackbird.

There are many kinds of bird feet. Take a look at figure 126. The top left foot is that of a perching bird. These make up the majority of our feathered chums. The foot, bottom left, is that of a golden eagle. This has to be strong with sharp talons to hold and kill prey. The top right drawing shows the foot of a woodpecker. This has evolved so that this bird can grip to bark

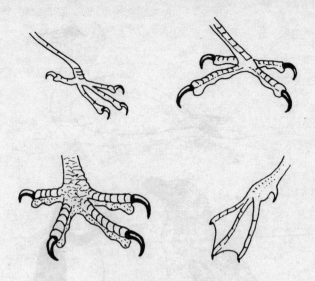

Fig. 126 Birds' feet.

tightly while it hunts for insects or hammers out a nesting hole. Woodpeckers don't give themselves nasty headaches because they have a brain which is suspended in liquid. You learn all sorts of things when you start out as a bird artist! The bottom right illustration is of a duck's webbed foot which, of course, is designed for paddling. Make notes of different feet.

It's nice for city dwellers to visit the sea in order to see exotic birds. I went to North Yorkshire to study and then sketch the birds you can see in figure 127. All these birds, plus hundreds more, were on the same crowded cliff face in the Royal Society for the Protection of Birds reserve at Bempton. It was nesting time. The gannet, top sketch, is a large bird with a wing span equal to the height of a tall man. It makes spectacular high speed dives straight into the sea when fishing. The razor bill, middle left (not to the same scale), hunts in a more sedate fashion. This is a darkly marked bird with white wing flashes. The little puffin, middle right, is a charming creature that is much persecuted by killer gulls and other predators. It has a large, multi-coloured bill for scooping up tiny sand eels. The gentle-looking bird at the bottom of figure 127 is a kittiwake. This pretty creature spends most of its life on the wing so it was great to be able to see it at close quarters. Notice the black-tipped wing and tail feathers. Scale up your drawing to copy these fine birds.

Fig. 127 A selection of seabirds.

Quackers

You need go no further than your local park pond, lake or stream to sketch the birds in figure 128. The top illustration is of a mallard duck coming in to land. Note the way it fans out its tail to act as a brake. It can also reverse the thrust of its wings to slow up. A handful of old bread crusts will soon bring a flock to you. You may have noticed that it is the male birds which are the most colourful or striking. This is because the females tend to be drab so that they blend in with their environment when nesting. Nature isn't silly is it?

Small dark birds are often to be found where there is water. The middle drawings of figure 128 are of a coot and a moorhen. People sometimes confuse the two. The coot, middle left, is a black bird with a white forehead and light beak. It is slightly

Fig. 128 Birds of pond, river and lake.

Fig. 129 Draw this kestrel.

larger than a moorhen, which has a red beak and legs, and white wing flashes with white under the tail, as in the drawing middle right. The tufted duck, bottom drawing, is black with white underparts. Draw your version of figure 128.

Falcons

Falconry is now a popular sport. It is possible to see some magnificent birds of prey in reserves and zoos. Some garden centres now have the added attraction of a falconry which may contain a wide collection of birds of prey. There is one little falcon, however, which all who use our motorways can see every few miles, though drivers mustn't allow themselves to be distracted from the road. The kestrel is the bird which hovers over motorway verges as it hunts for voles and insects. It is a very attractive creature. Look at the male kestrel I have drawn for figure 129. I sketched in each main feather shape before shading it in with close lines. Then the black markings were put in, with dot stipple used for the head feather markings. You can

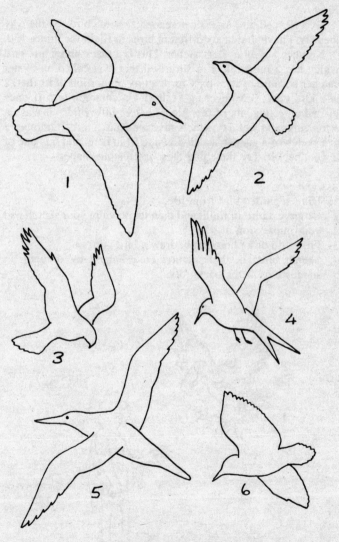

Fig. 130 Birds in flight.

make a nice picture of this by using a soft pencil. Most bird pictures, by the way, are much better done as paintings, but before you can paint you need to learn how to draw your subjects accurately. Copy the kestrel.

Flighty

Experienced bird artists can recognize some birds by the way they fly. I have drawn six different birds in flight for figure 130.

Number 1 is an oyster catcher. This is a black and white bird which has a red beak. I'm surprised that it is called an oyster catcher because oysters only form a tiny proportion of its diet. 2 is a kittiwake; 3 a hovering kestrel; 4 a common tern (I once visited a nesting site of this highly active little bird – it was on a freezing cold wet day which gave me quite a turn!); number 5 is a sketch of a gannet scaled down to fit in here; and 6 is one of a woodpecker. Try sketching these interesting shapes.

Assignments
1. Draw a garden bird from life.
2. Observe a bird in flight and then jot down in your sketch pad your impression of it.
3. From life or a photograph, draw a bird portrait.
4. Sketch birds in their natural environment by drawing in suggestions of the background.

18
Moving On To People

We see human faces everywhere we go, yet drawing them, to the beginner, seems a difficult task. Perhaps some folk expect instant skill and are therefore surprised to find it so. Unfortunately, however, the ability to produce life-like pictures can only come with practice and knowledge.

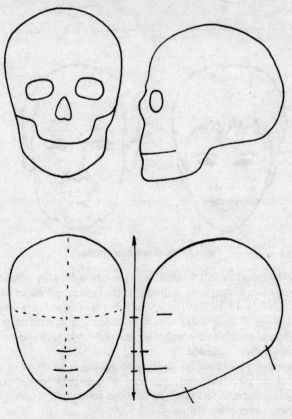

Fig. 132 The skull shape.

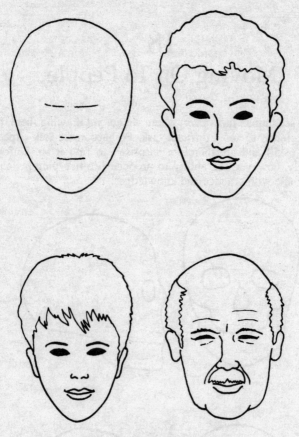

Fig. 133 Outlines first (frontal).

To be good at this branch of art is rewarding. A competent portraitist can soon have a queue of customers, all eager to part with fistfuls of money in exchange for a good drawing of themselves. People seem always to enjoy – and wish to own – an original portrait of which they are the subject. We are a vain lot, this author included.

Directly you show an ability for getting a likeness of your subject in your sketches, you can also expect invitations to parties, complete strangers to become immediate friends, and limitless other possibilities.

Remember: start by jotting down the accurate outline – don't bother with details until later.

Profile and frontal

It's vital to fix in your mind the basic shapes of a skull, front and side. Look at figure 132. Notice how the outlines can be simplified into sound structures on which to build a drawing.

Think of a head as being like an egg with the broad end on top (frontal view). Half way from the top to the bottom of this is where the eye line is. Then, half way between the eye and bottom of the jaw, is the underside of the nose. Half way between the end of the nose and the chin is where the mouth line should be.

Fig. 134 Basic shape first (profile).

The same guide applies to a head in profile, but the shape from the side is different because the skull extends further back. Looked at from the side the structure of a face is still rather like an egg but one with a flattened side. Notice how dotted lines, lightly drawn, will give you the correct positions for eyes, nose and mouth. And how the neck lines have also been marked on the example in figure 132. The neck does not pop straight up from the top of the body. It comes out at an angle which varies with each individual.

While these proportions give a fairly accurate form to work from, remember that faces vary; some have long jaws, or high foreheads, or narrow faces, and so on. Just as an egg is rounded so is a head. We soon discover the differences when we work. Take heart that, provided you start by putting down, in faint lines, the general outlines as I have just explained, your drawings will always be on the right track. This way only minor adjustments should be needed later.

See the faces in figure 133. Copy them – outlines first, remember! Next have a close look at the profile in figure 134, and do the same exercise.

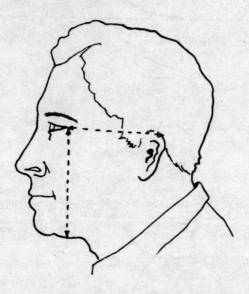

Fig. 135 Where the ear should go.

148

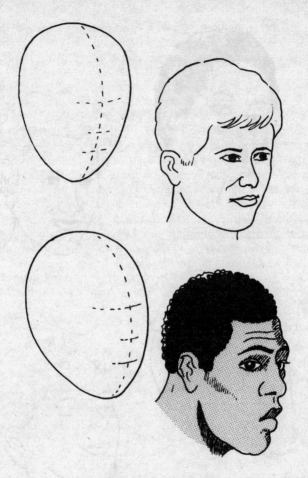

Fig. 136 The structure lines.

Ear here

A common mistake when drawing a face in profile is to put the ear in the wrong place. It's much further towards the back of the head than is often imagined. See figure 135. The distance from the outside corner of the eye to where the back of the ear comes, should be roughly equal to the space from there to the bottom of the jaw. This, of course, will vary slightly between individuals as do all other features. Now you have a little more knowledge to help you.

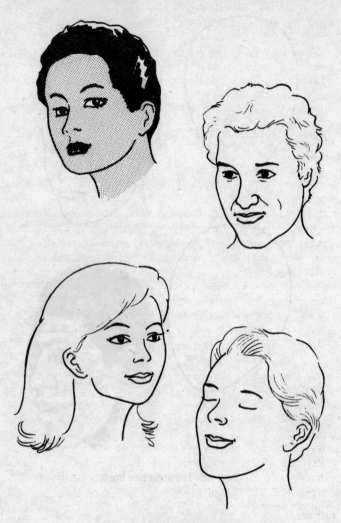

Fig. 137 A little more detail.

Turn your head

After practising frontal and profile sketches we move on to find out what to do when a face is *partly* turned. The drawing procedure is the same although we are seeing the person from an angle. Think of the egg shape and how those dotted frontal position-lines would give an illusion of a curve if the egg were turned; then build your drawing on the right structure, and you are winning. See figure 136. Although for the bottom head I used a printing technique for the purposes of publication, in the original drawing I shaded it in simply by using close, even lines, and blocked in the hair. Try this technique in pencil to begin with. Constantly remind yourself how the oval basic shape must vary slightly with each subject. Practise drawing your basic facial shapes using the finished illustrations in figure 137.

Bits and pieces

For now, don't worry about drawing too much detail in the face. We shall be dealing with this later on. One of the many things about recording the human face is the way we all differ from each other in every feature, identical twins excluded. No two mouths, noses, or even nostrils are the same. Each pair of eyes is unique. Most of us have uneven faces. One side is by no means symmetrical with the other. So the drawing job requires careful looking.

To stare at an intended subject can be disconcerting so it's better to practise, to begin with, on friends and relatives. You may find that they become rather rigid or shift about a lot. However, be patient; use your humour; then plod away. Your model will soon relax.

Lots of choice.

A good source of static models can be found in daily newspapers. Their pages are full of faces; however, many grin out at the reader. Avoid these, and try to sketch from the serious, or candid shots.

It is wonderful practice to wander about with a small pad and quickly jot down impressions. The drawings here were done with a drawing pen and black ink. However, you will find that a soft pencil makes the job simple, and you can obtain tone and texture to a very fine standard.

Assignments
1. Draw four frontal faces after putting down the basic shape.
2. Draw four profiles in a similar fashion.
3. Try four sketches of angled faces.

19
A Nose And A Bit Of Lip

We'll start with a reminder about how to sharpen your pencil. Rather than resort to a pencil sharpener, most artists prefer to use a knife or cutting blade to fashion the business end of the

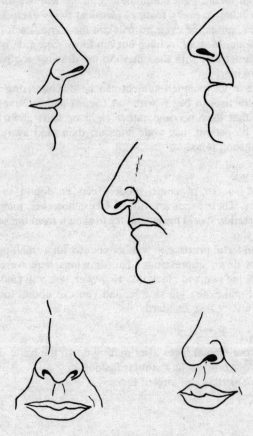

Fig. 138 Different noses.

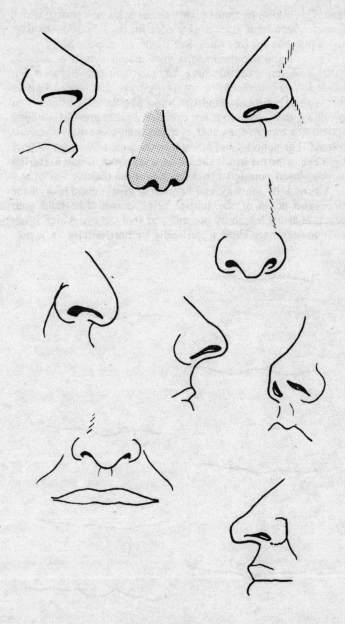

Fig. 139 Nostrils.

lead. This allows them to create a chisel point on a pencil, which is useful because it gives a wide edge for thick lines or shading, and a thin one for fine lines. See figure 70 on page 82.

The eye you use the most is your master eye. It is usual to have a master eye matching whether you are right or left handed. You can check the following way: hold a pencil up, in line with any vertical item (which could be the edge of a door or window); then close your left eye. See what happens. If nothing appears to move, open that eye and then close the other one instead. The pencil should then seem to jump to the right if your right eye is the master. It should have appeared to bolt to the left as you closed your left eye if that one is the master.

A pencil, by the way, can be used to give a good idea of the slope and angle of the subject being drawn. Just hold your pencil at arm's length by one end and shut the eye which is not your master one. Hold it vertically or horizontally as appro-

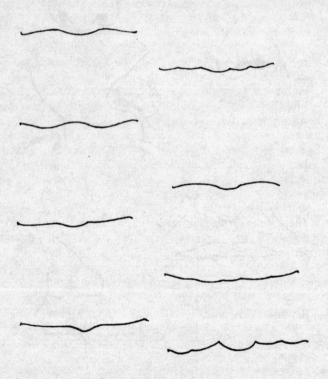

Fig. 140 Mouth lines are wavy.

priate. Squint along the straight line provided by your pencil against the subject. You can then see if the line which you want to draw is vertical, horizontal, or slopes. You now have another aid to successful drawing.

Nose construction

Once you are able accurately to draw facial features, the whole face can be undertaken with confidence. It is far simpler to break the job down into stages than to try to master the whole lot at once. The nose is the most obvious part of the face with which to start. Noses come in all sorts of shapes and sizes, as do cheeks and other bits of the face. Noses can be crooked, straight, droopy, Roman, Greek, small, long, thin, fat, or, well, just different! As usual, careful *looking* is required before putting pencil to paper.

Figure 138 gives examples taken from life. Notice how, whilst the overall shape of each nose varies considerably from person to person, the nostrils are essentially much the same. They mainly only differ according to the angle from which they are viewed. Copy these drawings with fast, bold lines and don't worry about mistakes. They will quickly disappear as you progress.

Figure 139 should give you more ideas on how our breathing apparatus can differ. Your own wonderful face – plus a mirror – will help you learn a great deal about a human face and about *looking* properly at a subject! Observe the way your nose is put together, how your nostrils appear as dark slots, and so on. Study these additional examples in figure 139; then draw them too.

A bit of lip

There are numerous different mouth shapes, and this feature changes with age. Figure 140 shows just the mouth line between upper and lower lip. You can see that there is never a straight line. Most lips are curvy, with a dip in the middle of the upper one. Mouths can also be uneven, one side being different from the other.

It's getting these small, and not so small, variations right that can turn a mediocre sketch into a genuine likeness. How do we get them right? By *looking!* Doing so properly becomes easy with practice.

Look at figure 141. These illustrations of lips reveal the way lips are creased by small lines which follow the curve of the flesh. The lines can be deep or faint, many or few, and they tend to be criss-crossed in the elderly. A tip worth remembering, however, is to leave out many of these marks. Otherwise the finished mouth can look like crazy-pavement.

Teeth are best left blank for the same reason. The artist who draws people resembling mutant creatures from a black swamp might have a future in horror comics but not as a sought-after portrait specialist. Maybe your in-laws do look like monsters to you but there's no need to depict them so. Be kind to your victims and they could be good to you!

Folk are quick to praise a good picture of themselves but quicker still to criticise a bad one, or one which ages them. Being accurate in drawing is all about being self-confident. Once you have become proficient at drawing the various parts of the face it is then relatively easy to attempt the whole. The time swiftly comes when you glimpse at an interesting face, say to yourself, "yes, I can draw that one", and you do! Get into the good habit of thinking positively and mentally sketching every face. Your progress will soon amaze you. YOU CAN LEARN TO DO ANYTHING.

Put them together

Take a step forward now, by drawing a nose and the mouth beneath it, as in the examples in figure 142. See the different angles. Try other views. Put in a little shading and a few facial lines. Notice how we have a groove running from our nostrils to the centre of our upper lip. This is drawn as a single line, two lines, or left blank, according to what is seen.

Observe yourself in a mirror to see how shadows fall. There is one shadow under the bottom lip, another under the droop of a nose.

Look at the way things are when a face is partly turned away from or towards you. If you use yourself as a model, as Vincent Van Gogh did many times, it will help you to have two or three mirrors handy. If you don't own more than one mirror don't worry; you are following in the footsteps of the now-famous poverty-striken impressionist. But there is no need to lop off an ear just yet – we shall be studying these bits in the next chapter. Wait until then!

Sketching noses and mouths is straightforward, and many quick drawings can be done in an hour or two. You may have discovered that, when drawings begin to improve, the subject becomes addictive and pictures simply pour out! Although

Fig. 141 Lips in detail.

157

Fig. 142 Different angles.

drawing-pads are not too expensive, a more economical material to use is good quality typing paper purchased by the ream (500 sheets).

I needed between 40 and 70 roughs and original drawings per chapter to produce this book. An output like this would use up an awful lot of sketch pads, so I worked on typing paper.

It's wise to churn out many drawings rather than to make just a few meticulous ones. Quite often a fast, spontaneous effort can't be bettered.

One of the reasons for copying the examples given is to help you to become quick and accurate and to draw with simple lines. Most beginners tend to try instead to put down every line. They end up with a mess. Experienced artists suggest form and shape with as few lines as possible. This makes for less work and an easier life, which is something we all aim for!

Assignments
1. Ask four people you know to pose for you. Draw their noses and mouths. If you live alone, or can't get about, use newspaper photographs.
2. See how many noses and mouths you can sketch in pencil within one hour. Model them on photos in magazines, catalogues, albums – wherever they may be close at hand.

20
Eyes And Ears

Eye, eye, eye

Drawing the eye needn't be as difficult as some newcomers to art make it. The part we see isn't round except in newly born babies. The bit we want to sketch is shuttered by upper and lower lids, and is fringed with eye lashes. It's the surrounding pieces which confuse and tend to put beginners off. The answer to the problem is to study and learn to draw each item, one at a time.

As with all facial features, with eyes there is a great variety – without which we would be a pretty boring lot. The examples in figure 143 cover both sexes and a range of ages. The actual shape of most eyes is rather like a tear drop laid on one side. The one common factor we see is the duct at the inner corner of each eye.

Notice the differences in eyelids; they can be thick, thin, heavy, bulging or hardly visible. The lower lid usually shows a rim from which fine lashes sprout.

Bags beneath eyes cast a tiny shade. Just as the chin throws a deep shadow on the neck, the brow causes eyes to be indistinct.

We all favour one of our eyes, the master eye, and this has an effect on its lid as we grow up. As a result, when we study grown-up people, few have a perfectly matching pair.

Ladies have prettier peepers than men as a rule, and they can enhance their long lashes with make-up. This helps to make the drawing of their eyes a little bit easier.

The size of the pupil (the dark circle in the middle) varies according to the light, and the vision of the person concerned. When drawing eyes remember to leave a white spot on the pupil. This is reflected light which gives life to an eye. The area immediately surrounding the pupil (the iris), is drawn by fine lines which radiate out. Dark eyes are recorded by dense shading or are blocked in.

Try sketching the eye shapes from figure 143, until you can quickly put down accurate copies. This task should take all of ten minutes for a confident person like you. Then add lids and

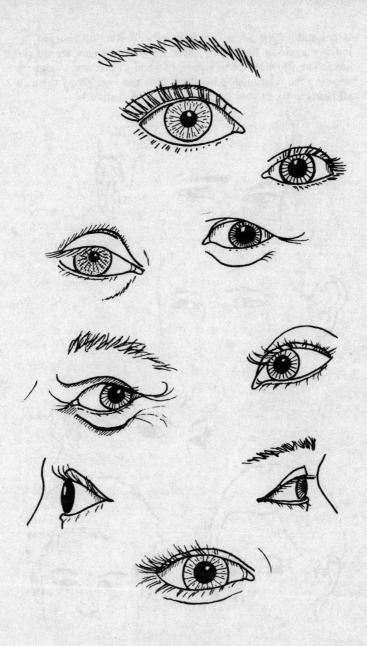

Fig. 143 Eye close-ups.

lashes and maybe a few face lines as well. Remind yourself, by looking again at figure 135, how far back the ears are on the head. The illustrations in figure 144 add to that knowledge by showing the relationship between eyes and ears. Copy them; it all helps to fix in your mind the way each feature is.

Fig. 144 Position of the eyes.

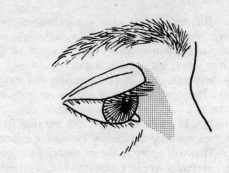

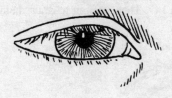

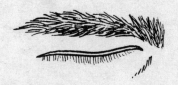

Fig. 145 Close-up details.

The eye in figure 145 is that of a nice young man who agreed to act as a model. See in the top view how the hair of the eyebrow has been drawn, fine lines running the way it actually grows. The upper eyelid extends either side beyond the surface of the eyeball. The lashes curve gently up from the top lid, but are sparse on the lower one. The tear duct can just be seen at the inner end of the eye.

The middle picture, in figure 145, will give you more clues on how to draw eyelashes.

The bottom view of the closed eye shows the fringe of lashes, and how the shut lid is sketched as just two thin lines. The eyebrow also pulls down nearer to the eye.

Alas, when we become older it all changes. See figure 146. Your keen observation will take in the bags, lines, straggly eyebrows, and thinning lashes. No, it's not an illustration of your author's eye; his is much worse!

Copy these examples, in pencil, using thin and thick lines as necessary. Then go over your masterpieces with a fibre-tip pen just so that you can see what each medium does.

You should be aware that most folk are seen from a distance, and that their eyes are not clearly visible but appear just as dark shadows. This will apply to the majority of subjects you sketch from life, around town, in a supermarket, or wherever they may be. Bear this in mind. It will save many mistakes and much time if eyes are simply blocked in as in the early figures here. It's possible to do this and still obtain a good likeness. Take a careful peep at the people in figure 147. Then attempt to draw them.

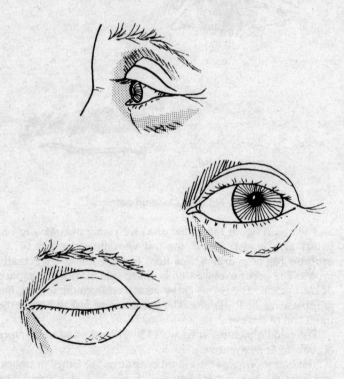

Fig. 146 Detailed eyes.

Fig. 147 Blocked in eyes.

Glasses

   With age eyesight deteriorates, and most of us eventually trudge off to an optician, later to emerge self-consciously wearing spectacles. At least they help us to see our victim in sharp focus again!

   Sketching glasses is quite simple but it is exacting. You need to practise a little technical draughtsmanship. There are countless frame designs around to observe. It's best to sketch the frames only, and leave out the eyes unless a close-up portrait is being made. Study the specs in figure 148; then copy them.

Fig. 148 Notice the different types of frame.

Ear we go again!

Ears are very interesting to draw because each person has a unique pair. Some are easy to jot down but others require much thinking about and a lot of *looking*. The ear is dish-like, with a turned-over rim designed to catch sound and channel it down to the ear canal. They come in all sorts of sizes (and abilities to listen!), with many variations of the basic shape, and they may well have unexpected lumps and ridges.

166

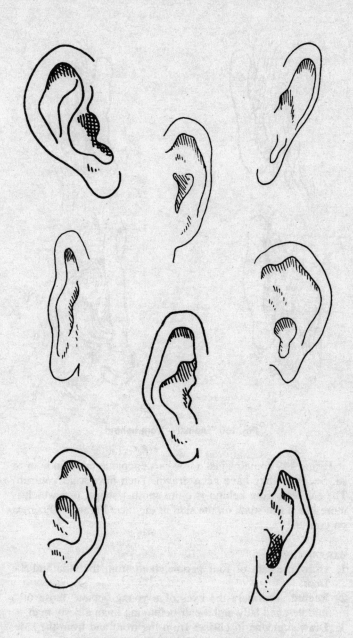

Fig. 149 A selection of ears.

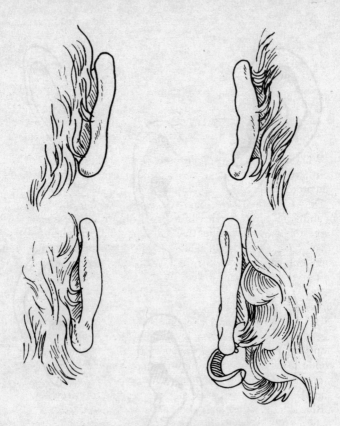

Fig. 150 The ear – from behind.

Figure 149 contains just a few ears encountered in an hour or so. See how they have been drawn. Then have a go yourself. The ear seen from behind is quite another shape, one which is more like a rim stuck on the side of the face. Figure 150 is next on your list.

Assignments
1. Draw the ears of four people, both from the side and the front.
2. Record accurately the eyes of a young person, those of a middle-aged lady and a pair belonging to an elderly man.
3. Draw someone in glasses from the front and from the side. In this exercise do not bother about other features.

21
Bring On The Wig

What a magnificent range of hair styles there are – artistic, weird, tangled, wild, neat, and glorious. Some of those worn by men aren't bad either!

Drawing hair at close-quarters requires keen observation and an ability to simplify what is seen. Mostly it will be a matter of suggesting a fashion rather than of meticulous draughtsmanship. If you have a wonderful thatch and a mirror then you have an immediate model – you. If, like this author, your personal prop isn't up to much, then bring on the wig, or use friends.

Different styles

Have a look at the styles in figure 151. The top left one is of a gentleman with silver, wavy locks which have been created simply by means of a few lines, like those of the long-haired blonde opposite him. Shadows are depicted by slightly increasing the number of lines. This is more noticeable in the example of a pony-tail style as in the middle left drawing.

Black or very dark hair should not be drawn as a solid mass. It's best to leave highlights in as shown on the other illustrations in figure 151.

Three of the hair styles in figure 152 have been produced by pen *and* brush. The broken, rough line effect is achieved by what is known as a dry brush technique. A fairly thick drawing ink is used on a small, good quality paint brush. This is first loaded with ink, and then most of the contents are wiped off on a piece of scrap paper. When the bristles are almost dry the brush is dragged across the area of the picture as required. The result is rather like that obtained with charcoal, which is also an excellent medium for portraits and figures. A similar effect can be achieved with a soft pencil on rough-surfaced cartridge-paper. It's one of the tricks of the trade and is useful on many other subjects besides humans.

Points to remember when sketching hair are that it reflects strong lights and has several degrees of tone. Those go from

Fig. 151 Sketch various hair styles.

dense black through medium grey to white. It will help your
progress to copy the examples in figures 151 and 152.

170

Crowning glory

Perhaps you are old enough to recall how the Beatles mop-head style swept round the world, and wasn't just confined to young men? Today, although the older generation may tend to stick to the same thatch, luckily there are thousands of youngsters who certainly do not. This makes our job much more interesting. Young ladies especially, may change their hair styles

Fig. 152 Use pen and brush.

Fig. 153 Sketch fine hair.

frequently. Some of them grow marvellous tresses which at first glance might appear to be difficult to draw. In practice it's a straight-forward task of calling for patience and proper *looking*. Figure 153 is of such a model. The illustration took a little time due to having to put down masses of fine lines, most of which were curved and ran the way the locks fell. There are plenty of medium and dark tones, but a lot of the white paper was allowed

172

to show through. Study all aspects of this example. Then draw your version. You will draw a basic shape first won't you?

You should now turn your attention to the men's heads in figure 154. The technique is just the same but there's less hair. The pen drawing at the top of this page is of a man with curly, dark hair. Notice how the waves have been recorded, and the way the lines go back at the sides of the head.

The illustration beneath is of a man with light coloured locks which are swept across the head. Not quite as much pen work is needed here. Try these as your next project.

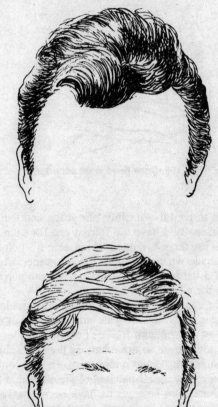

Fig. 154 Draw male hair styles.

Fig. 155 Draw head wear accurately.

Head gear

Hats seem to go out of fashion for years, and then suddenly reappear. Personally, I have a different one for each day of the week. Artists use them for practical reasons: it's helpful to have the eyes in shade when working outdoors, especially in strong sunlight and a hat keeps the head cool in summer but retains body heat in the winter.

Head wear can vary from a knotted handkerchief, through scarves, shades, caps, to full-scale productions that resemble a hanging basket packed with fruit or flowers.

It makes good sense to draw hats as the sole subject before attempting to sketch people under them. Have a look at figure 155 and notice how small patches of shading help to give an illusion of shape. See how seams have been clearly inscribed. It's useful to be able to draw head gear from all angles – which is how we see folk wearing hats.

A common error for beginners to make is to draw the lid too big or too small, so that the head does not appear to fit into it the right way. The material in a hat is usually thin and follows the lines of the head very closely.

Figure 156 demonstrates how a brim can conceal eyebrows and sometimes eyes too. A peak can throw a strong shadow across the front of a face, as in the sketch at the top. The hat may have a brim which sags down unevenly. Capturing that jaunty angle (of hat) is all about *looking*, yet again.

Fig. 156 Different types of hat.

Assignments
1. Make two accurate sketches of hair styles of a girl and of a young man.
2. Draw the hair of two older people.
3. Picture four different types of hat. People two of them.

22
Hands And Feet

Most beginner artists draw hands and feet far too small and incorrectly. Surprisingly, it's a common fault with more experienced artists too. A tip to help you avoid this is to remember that a hand, from palm base to fingertips, is as long as a face. Compare yours now. A foot is bigger still. It measures slightly more than the length of the entire head. Don't try to check yours without a ruler or you may do yourself an injury!

Students don't spend enough time *looking* properly or practising drawing these extremities. They may seem difficult to draw but really they are no harder to do than other parts of the human body. We can use ourselves or friends as models, so there is no problem finding different examples.

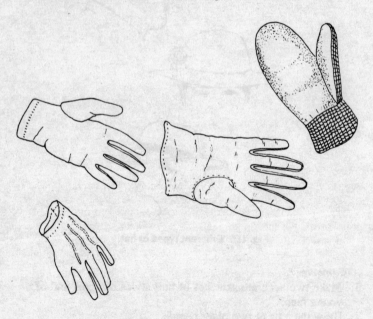

Fig. 157 Gloves are hand-like.

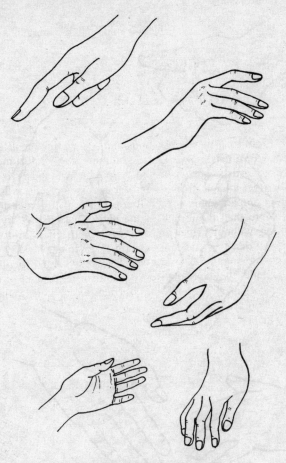

Fig. 158 The female hand.

Be handy

Sketching gloves is a simple way to start learning how to draw hands. The basic shape of a hand is similar to a mitten. They are easy to draw. See figure 157. Ladies' gloves are usually made to fit more exactly over fingers and hand than gentlemen's ones. Note how hand-like gloves are, and after studying the ink stipple and fine lines of figure 157, have a shot at copying these examples accurately.

You can use your non-drawing hand as a model. A mirror will enable several angles to be viewed, then drawn. The back of the

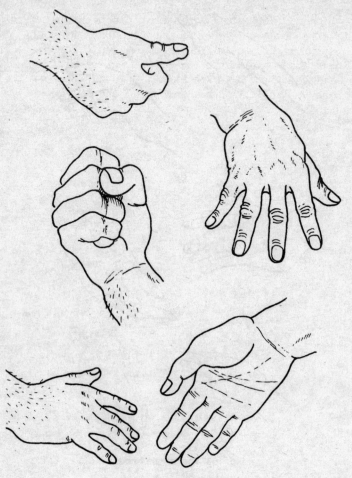

Fig. 159 Men's hands.

hand, you will discover, is gently curved in convex fashion, while the underside is concave. The fingers follow a shallow curve from the top of the palm. There are three finger joints which show as lines, but these do not correspond exactly, because of the fingers having different lengths. The cushions at each fingertip vary from person to person, and knuckles may be prominent or barely seen. Old hands carry wrinkles on the fingers and the backs of the hand, but it isn't necessary to try to put them all in.

By now you should be wise and experienced enough to know that the idea is to *suggest* rather than laboriously attempt to get down every tiny detail. You probably don't need telling that there is a big difference between the soft, usually beautiful hands of girls and the rough, blunt-fingered hairy paws of men. Examine the illustrations in figures 158 and 159. Then copy them in pencil or fibre-tip pen.

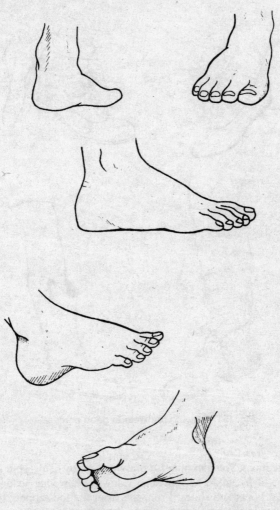

Fig. 160 The foot – from different angles.

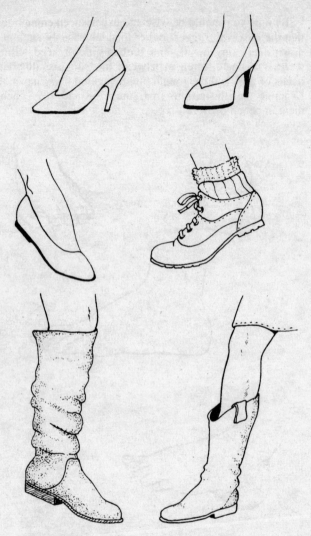

Fig. 161 Drawing footwear is good practice.

Best foot forward

Once more, you can practise drawing feet by using your own or those of friends. The foot seen sideways is wedge shaped as are most boots and shoes. From the front the toes appear to be broad due to them being nearest to the beholder. (That's called perspective.) However, viewed from above, the toes seem to be pointed or narrow. The same applies to footwear and this is an important point to remember when sketching.

The marvellous human foot is constructed in the form of a series of arches which make it super strong, flexible and able to

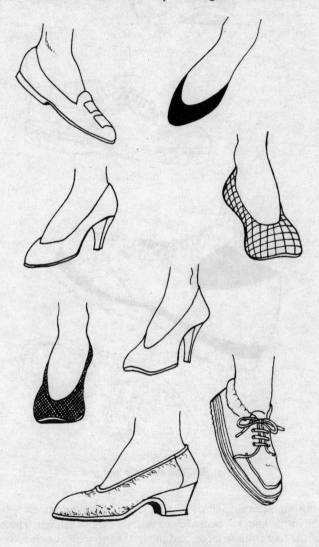

Fig. 162 Popular styles.

Fig. 163 The author's foot gear.

withstand constant shock. Ankle joints protrude from each side, the inside knuckle being lower than its outside partner. The ball of the foot is quite large, and the heel is no midget either. Study figure 160 and copy.

Get your shoes on

Practically all the folk you will be drawing will be wearing footwear of some kind, so it is logical to learn how to draw these items. Sketching footwear is good for improving observation and drawing techniques.

Ladies have a huge range of styles to choose from, and fashions change, sometimes quite fast. The court shoe, however, seems to be ever popular. Look at those at the top of figure 161. Apart from the possible addition of bows, bells, and from their colours, they remain pretty much the same year in and year out. Note how the heel bulges out and then sweeps down to the toe position.

Boots are fashionable. Flat heeled shoes are quite common with leisure dress, and sports shoes abound. Figure 162 shows more styles.

See how all these examples have been drawn. Your eagle eye will pick out the way the foot arches out of a shoe, and the way ankles appear from side and front.

Footwear is made from many materials. These figures show how dot stippling and other techniques can be employed to suggest what has been used.

Men's footwear has undergone many changes in the past decade, but there are still scores of styles which haven't altered very much. A good way to start on footwear is to dig out your own and draw what you find, as I did for the examples in figure 163. The sketch at the top of the page was produced having placed a mirror opposite my feet. Most of us have a favourite pair or two of shoes; those depicted happen to be mine – worn out and the despair of repairers far and wide!

Old boots and shoes tend to be nicer to draw because of age lines, bumps and bulges – it sounds a bit like sketching faces doesn't it? When looking at your own foot gear, work out how you are going to suggest the fabric used before you mark your paper. And note carefully where the seams will show. Experienced artists develop these habits to the point they no longer have to remind themselves to follow them.

Assignments
1. Draw two pages of hands, your own and friends'.
2. Do the same with feet, and footwear.
3. Draw six old and six modern shoe styles.

23
Arms And Legs

Ladies, of course, come first, so I will start on their lovely flowing lines. Members of the fairer sex have more flexible elbows than men so we can see in them poses which fellows can't equal. Female arms hang closer to the body than those of men, and their forearms are slightly shorter than those of the male. This is probably due to early man being the hunter, having to hurl a spear about, club enemies, and lift heavy rocks.

The arm is quite long, and the old yard measurement may have been based on this fact. If you stand up and drop your arms down you will find that your fingertips reach the middle of your thighs. If your hands are level with your ankles you're an ape, but don't worry, chimps can learn to draw!

Take a peep at figure 164. See how the upper arm is shorter than the forearm. All women have a layer of fat beneath their skin, which is responsible for their smooth, streamlined shape compared to men. Copy the illustrations. Then draw the arms of ladies around and about.

Muscle power

Figure 165 shows the ripples, bulges and potential power seen in a man's arm. Note the pronounced shoulder muscle, and the biceps and upper arm which are designed to bend the limb. The triceps in the lower arm are usually obvious too, and most fellows have hairs on their arms and hands. Try to remember how the arm looks from either side, as well as from the front and rear. This will help you with future work.

On with the sleeves

Most folk you will sketch will be clothed, so you need to spend time and thought on how to draw their garments. Ladies, bless them, expose their arms and legs far more than chaps, but you must still learn how to use a pen or pencil to depict material, as part of your apprenticeship. So, indoors or outside, get into the habit of observing the way clothes hang, crease and fold. It's

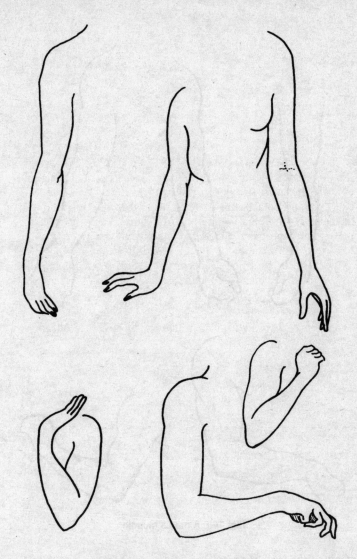

Fig. 164 Smooth ladies' arms.

all about *looking*, isn't it?

Figure 166 is of covered arms. The top left sketch shows a leather jacket, with the arm of an anorak opposite. The bottom two designs are of women's clothes, a coat and a blouse sleeve.

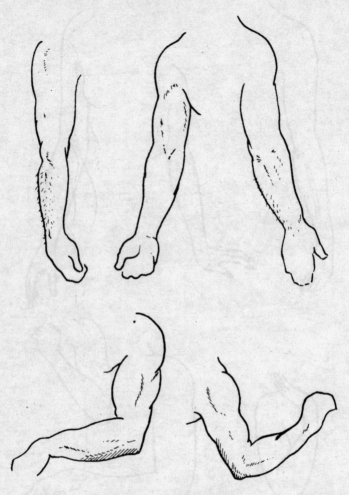

Fig. 165 A man's muscle.

Getting the legs 'together'

The length of a leg is roughly half the body's height. Some ladies, particularly model types, exceed this measurement and are much in demand in the advertising field. The legs of a model were used in figure 167. Notice the nice smooth, curved contours. These are best drawn in one sweeping motion. Look at the two small bumps which depict the knee cap, then at the tiny

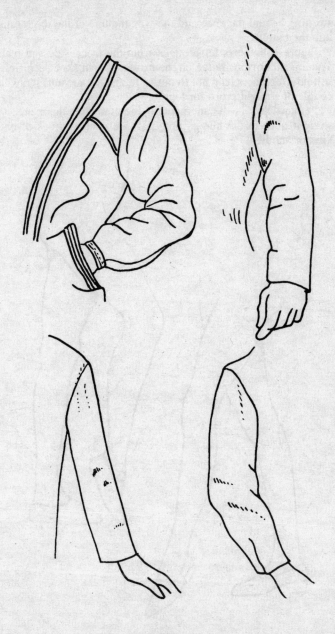

Fig. 166 Different sleeves.

swelling behind the knee and the way the line of the thigh runs into the buttock.

Figure 168 shows female legs from the front, side and rear. There is an obvious bulge on the inside of each knee seen from behind. Beginners tend not to notice it, and, as a result, scrawl a couple of straight props for legs.

Perhaps this is the moment to mention that there are *no* straight lines in the human body; all are gentle curves of one kind or another.

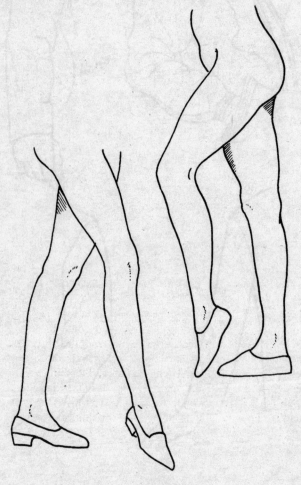

Fig. 167 A model's legs.

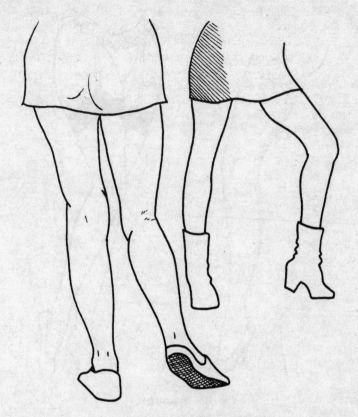

Fig. 168 Legs from different angles.

Stocking tops

Stockings are supposed to be making a come back against tights. Did your author hear three cheers from the older lads?

These pretty garments are nice to draw and come in many shades, styles and designs. There are the kind that are held up by suspenders and a belt, and some that need *no* bits and pieces to stay put. Isn't science wonderful? Figure 169 gives an example of each. Note the way the roundness of the thigh is followed by the line of the stocking top.

Power pins

Men's legs are shown in figure 170. It's noticeable how the appearance of thigh and calf muscles is not subdued by a layer

Fig. 169 Stockings.

of fat as in girls. That feminine padding, by the way, protects them from cold, and minor ailments, and is believed to be a factor in longevity. Is there no justice?

Sportsmen tune up their muscles and thus help an artist to see what's what. Glance at figure 171; then try copying the two athletes. The back pages of most newspapers contain many photographs of sporting gentlemen you can draw, whether they may be whacking a cricket ball, kicking a football, or punching someone's head.

To expand your work on this chapter you can find numerous models around you to dash off onto your action-pad. Draw a basic shape first. Don't stop at legs – include body, arms, hands and heads. We'll have no lolling about, drinking cups of tea, or watching TV during this important stage in your rapid progress. However, you may pause to whistle a happy tune before setting about the assignments!

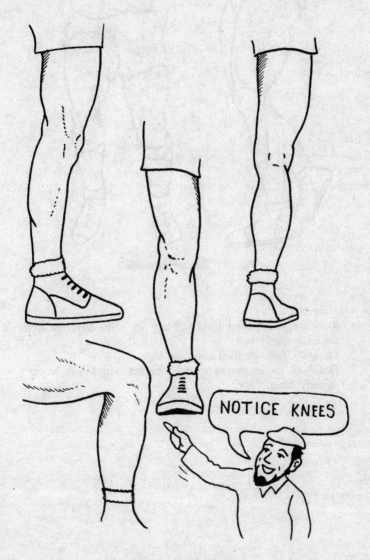

Fig. 170 Men's pins.

Fig. 171 Sportsmen's legs.

Assignments
1. Sketch four exposed arms and legs in poses different from the examples given.
2. Draw six fully-clothed arms and legs.
3. Draw all the examples in this chapter which you haven't already done.

24
The Torso And Big End

Almost all artists have an eye for a beautiful body, but not many beginners have the opportunity, or perhaps the confidence, to attend a life drawing class to learn this skill. If this applies to you don't worry. There are other ways of learning how to sketch the human figure. The female form is the one most used, published, drawn or painted. The male frame, in comparison, is rather plain and not nearly as curvaceous.

Stone Age artists depicted their women folk as having huge buttocks. We now believe that this was the way they actually were. When mankind first stopped crawling about and stood up, the powerful gluteal muscles were responsible for holding up the body weight. Since then the human form has changed and continues to alter. Modern woman has evolved to own narrower hips, a deeper, flatter tummy and generally quite pronounced, rounded breasts. She no longer looks like a cave woman – thank goodness.

A thing of beauty

There's more to drawing the female figure than there is to doing that of a man. The female torso and posterior, for example, often seem heavier, in size, than their male counterparts, due to the layer of fatty tissue women carry. Figure 172 gives the basic structure of a front pose, then the sketch. Below are back and profile views.

When we were children our elders said: "sit up straight", or "stand up straight". They were impossible requests because the human spine is curved, as you can see from my illustration. You will also spot the way the neck leaves the upper trunk at a distinct angle, as I mentioned in an earlier chapter. Notice too, the mass of muscle in buttocks and hips, and how the belly curves gently out. These are all important points to remember when you are drawing people.

If you draw over- and under-weight people first, you will learn rapidly the extent to which bodies differ. My subjects here were normal healthy types. Nevertheless, you can see how each

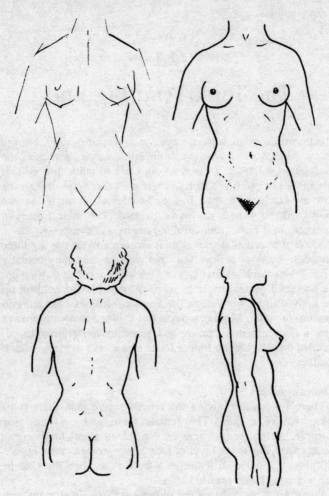

Fig. 172 Draw beautiful bodies.

part is unique to the individual, just as facial features are. Breast shape, for example, varies considerably between women and also according to age. Perfection in this department happens in the late teens when bosoms are firm and round. From then on mammary glands become heavier and gravity pull causes them to sag.

Ladies undulate and sway when moving. This affects their shape and gives us artists problems, but ones which we can

194

confidently solve. Figure 173 shows a girl's back with her hips tilted, and this makes the buttock shape slightly different from the previous example. The basic construction lines show the subtle changes. This is why an accurate outline sketch is so vital.

Today, on many sunny holiday beaches, young ladies can be seen topless, like the example in figure 173. Mass-circulation daily papers carry so-called pin up photographs of well-endowed young models. Books on photography and art can provide other sources. So there is no shortage of subjects available for practice.

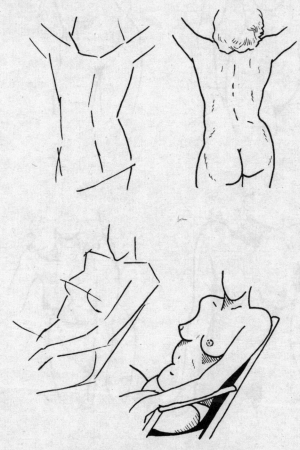

Fig. 173 Notice the construction lines.

Study each body in figure 174. Note how just a little fine pen shading can emphasise breast, belly and hip shapes. Look at the way bosoms are from different angles. The female belly is more

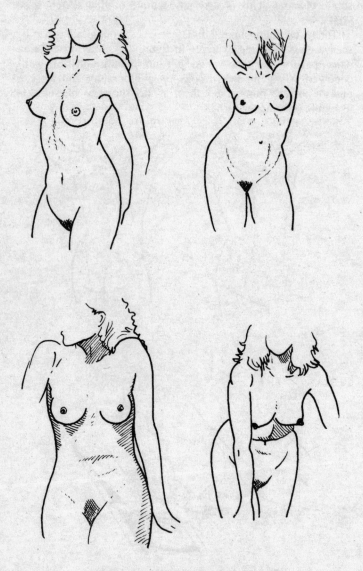

Fig. 174 See how fine shading works.

rounded than a man's. A torso can be long, short, fat or thin; a waist may be high, low or average. In these examples you can see a midline depression running from navel to lower chest. This is caused by side muscles meeting, and has been suggested by shading in the drawings. This line is not visible in the old or the overweight.

You can use yourself as a model with the aid of a full-length or large mirror – why not? Many famous artists churn out self-portraits. Vincent Van Gogh, as we all know, recorded his own anguished face regularly. I have been tempted to immortalise my own battered mug and gaunt frame but, to date, I haven't got round to actually doing it. Be thankful for small mercies!

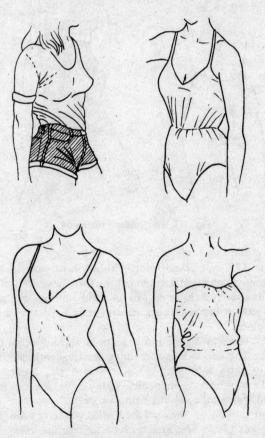

Fig. 175 Clothes show form.

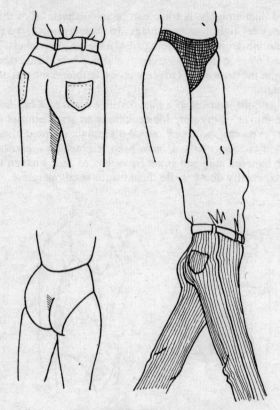

Fig. 176 The clothed backside.

Put the clothes on

Figure 175, of clothed figures, shows how material can be drawn to give the viewer an idea of the form beneath it. Creases and folds usually help to do this. A swim suit makes the body easy to sketch because this garment irons out lines, sags and small bulges.

Take a squint at figure 176 to learn how the covered bottom is drawn. The backside is something we frequently see. So it's useful to carry a small (A6) size sketch pad around when shopping or observing humanity. Lots of practice can then be obtained without the victims being aware.

Before moving on, draw all the bodies you have been looking at in figures 172 to 176. Start with basic structure lines, then jot down complete forms.

The male body

Figure 177 illustrates the average male torso, and, below, that of a boxer who has had to develop powerful hitting muscles in arms, back, chest and shoulders. The same over-development occurs in those individuals who, in sports jargon, pump iron.

Notice the clearly defined muscles each side of the midline depression, the narrow hips, wide shoulders and bulging muscles. You can see how these specimens look from the rear in figure 178. Note the curved spine. Body hair is suggested by short fine lines. Isn't it easy when you know how to do it?

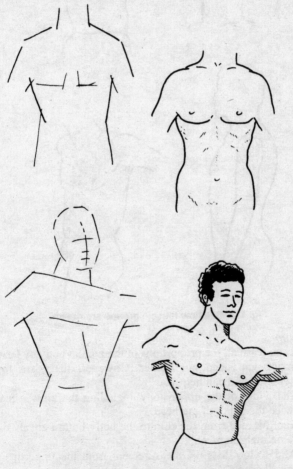

Fig. 177 Draw the construction lines first.

199

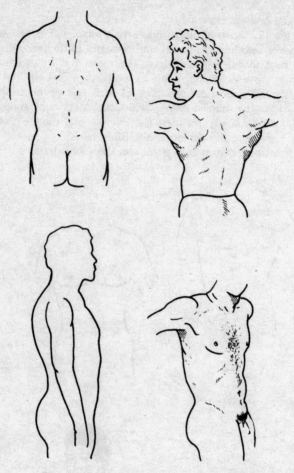

Fig. 178 See how muscle groups are drawn.

Proportions

You can learn all the proportions of the human body by heart. In practice you need not bother. However, there are four measurements that can help you:

1. The width of the upper body, including the arms, equals twice the depth of the head.
2. The distance from the chin to the belly-button equals that same measurement.
3. And so too does the measurement from the fingertips to the elbow.

4. The distance from the back of the neck to the bottom of the buttocks equals the depth of three heads.

These proportions vary slightly from person to person, but are a good guide. After experience is gained it's possible to judge if a drawing is right by just looking at it. Use bald head depths. You will go wrong if you include hair. I will give you a few more, useful measurements in the next chapter.

Throw some togs on

No matter how loose clothing is, it has to be drawn as if it covers a sturdy frame – which it does. Stripes on a shirt, sleeves or trunks can aid us to record shape. See figure 179. Notice the way creases and folds run. They may be curved – pulled down or up – but are always forced out of line by prominent parts of the body.

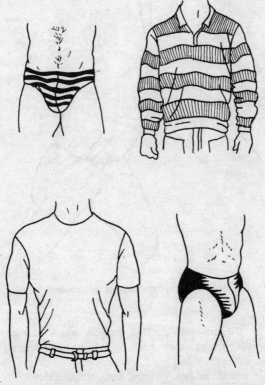

Fig. 179 Pay attention to creases and folds.

201

Drawing a motionless naked model can become rather dull and is very hard work. The covered form can be more exciting and erotic than a nude one. Getting out to draw the revolting peasants is lots of fun!

Sitting unseen in a café, art gallery, or library sketching people as they relax is rewarding and super practice. It's also the fastest way of becoming a good artist; try it.

The action men, in figure 180, show the way clothes can suggest power and movement. The sporting pages of newspapers will provide dozens of photographs of subjects in lots of different sports wearing a wide range of gear. Save a few old copies for practice but don't limit yourself to just one torso and big end; go for the whole figure. You can do it.

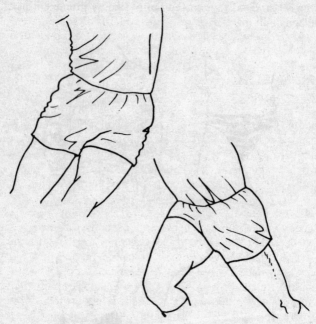

Fig. 180 How clothes suggest movement.

Assignments
1. Return to the drawings in this section which you haven't already copied, and tackle each one. I need not remind you how to *start* every time!
2. Draw six female bodies, clothed and unclothed.
3. Sketch six action drawings from newspaper cuttings.

25
Put It All Together

We draw best that which we know. It follows that to be good at drawing people some knowledge of anatomy is necessary. By doing the suggested exercises in past chapters you have been gaining this know-how, so you already have a good idea of how arms, legs, bodies, and other parts are constructed. Therefore, putting it all together should now be fairly straightforward.

A soft pencil such as a 4B is useful for figure drawing. Charcoal (which is burnt wood) is also excellent. Charred twigs were used by early caveman artists and still remain a common tool for the modern craftsman. Today, however, most artists' charcoal comes in smoothly prepared sticks. They give a dense black, with the ability also to create graduated tones that help you obtain a flesh-like effect on areas of skin. It smudges very readily but finished work can be fixed with an art or a hair spray. Sprays should be lightly used. It is wise to apply them from a distance rather than close-up.

Copying is an aid to successful drawing

Throughout these pages I have asked you to copy the illustrations. Almost all beginner artists start off this way, and you shouldn't think of this as cheating. Copying is valuable because it teaches you how to *look* properly and how to draw accurately – the basis of good art. A first class copy of a drawing requires great ability. Drawing from life, in fact, is copying what is seen. The big difference is all in the mind; the degree of self-confidence is different – that's all. After experience has been gained, copying is replaced by working from life or doing your own thing.

The nude model

You might not have a spouse, relative or friend willing to shed their threads, and life drawing classes may be out of reach; however, as I suggested earlier, photographs can provide an alternative source of subjects to work from.

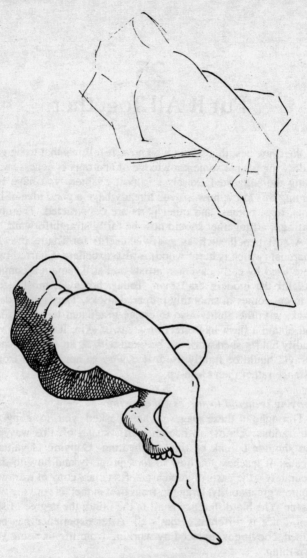

Fig. 181 Draw an unusual pose.

The model in figure 181 was drawn from life. The pose was unusual, with dark shadows, and had the appearance of being a headless body. First the basic structure was put down in pencil. Then the drawing was able to be done quickly with pen. Notice the curved lines in the cross-hatching. You could try this in pencil, or charcoal if you wish to extend your skills. If the latter is used, don't try to smudge it with the fingers; work with clean, bold strokes.

The model in figure 182 sits in a pose common in life classes, and is fairly easy to draw. Shoulder, arm and spine have been mapped out in the basic sketch. Many kinds of shadow effects can be achieved in any studio which has a variety of lights.

Fig. 182 An easy pose to draw.

Interesting pictures showing a range of dark and light tones are made possible.

Figure 183 is not hard to draw. Try this one in ink or fibre-tip pen. See how the shading has been done.

Fig. 183 Notice the shading.

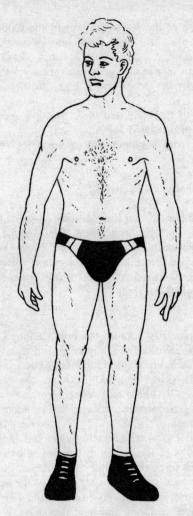

Fig. 184 Knowing proportions will help you.

More, useful measurements

As previously mentioned, beginners tend to draw feet and hands too small, but you will have mastered this now – right? Good for you!

Here are the additional guides to proportions which I promised to give you. All the measurements relate to the depth of the bald head:

1. From the top of the leg to the sole of the foot equals 3$^1/_2$ times the depth of the head. This can be 4 times, or longer, in a model.
2. From knee to sole of foot accounts for two of those heads.
3. The length of the upper arm is equal to the depth of the head.
4. The length of the hand and wrist together approximately equals that of one head depth.
5. The body, from shoulder top to the soles of the foot, usually stands 6$^1/_2$ heads tall, but it can go beyond 7 in some people.
6. Hips are usually 1$^1/_2$ heads wide.

It's possible to construct a line drawing of the human figure just by knowing what the proportions should be. The man in figure 184 was drawn this way. It could be worthwhile for you to try this. When you sketch a standing figure it will help you to refer back to the previous chapters, on arms, legs and bodies, as well, in order to get them right.

Clothed models

As we don't normally venture out into a naturist world our subjects are wearing clothes of many kinds and styles. It's super practice to draw as many fashion models as you can, male and female. The mini-skirt, invented back in the sixties, still regularly appears. (Did I hear more cheers from lads and lassies of all ages?) Young people wear a weird and wonderful range of clothes worth drawing.

Magazine and newspaper advertisements and junk mail, all contain photographs of models from which you can work, and you will gain much through learning how to depict smart clothes and how to draw good-to-look-at specimens of the human race.

Study the illustrations in figures 183, 186 and 187. Cast your eye over the simple fashions and how they have been drawn. Pay attention to figure shapes; then copy each drawing in pencil, before trying them again with a fibre-tip pen, charcoal, or whatever you fancy.

Assignments
1. Draw all the illustrations which you have yet to try in this section.
2. Produce four full-length drawings of relatives or friends.
3. Draw six fashion figures, male and female.

Fig. 185 Use simple lines.

Fig. 186 Copy this one.

210

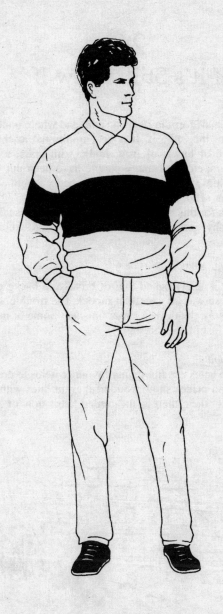

Fig. 187 Use blocking in.

211

26
If It's Still, Draw It

Still life is an art form in its own right, and whole books have been devoted to this subject. It is very traditional to churn out the odd picture of bowls of fruit, bottle with glass, tea cups, vases of flowers, etc., but many people have been put off this fascinating pastime by having the subject badly taught or thrust at them when at school.

The subjects for this book have been chosen because they can be used in many general pictures, and are good exercises as well.

Don't eat it first

I found that a newly baked loaf of bread as a background to a hunk of cheese was an excellent model. The trouble was that it got eaten before the drawing was finished. Some of us artists are greedy, or just plain starving!

Collect old wood

Old wooden gates are among my favourite items to draw. The ancient bars and pieces show wonderful grain lines with lots of different tones, then there's the added attraction of bygone

Fig. 188 Old wooden gates and posts make attractive drawings.

Fig. 189 Try collecting driftwood to sketch.

craftsmanship that went into the making of them. Today, of course, many new gates are made of steel, which isn't nice to look at, but it's cheaper and lasts longer than wood. With old gates there are usually equally elderly posts which are lovely to sketch. See figure 188, then try drawing it, or better still, go out and find one to draw from life.

Dead tree stumps, fence posts, roots and branches are other subjects which are easy to draw. Driftwood that has been cleaned by river or sea then bleached by the sun is attractive to sketch. Some shops sell pieces of this as highly varnished, highly priced ornaments. The branch shown in figure 189 was found on the banks of an estuary. It's very useful indeed to keep ink sketches of objects such as this because they can be added to pictures to improve composition or fill in gaps. See how fence posts add a little to the drawings in figures 190 and 191.

I use a fine pointed pen for this work and have found that by decreasing finger pressure on the pen, very thin, delicate lines

Fig. 190 Improve the composition of your drawing by adding fence posts.

213

Fig. 191 An old wooden fence can add something to a picture.

Fig. 192 Bits of bark, cracks and knots in the wood can be most effective.

can be produced. This is a help in recording, for example, the fine lines of wood grain, or those seen in leaves or flowers. Examine the posts in figures 192 and 193. Bits of bark, cracks and knots in the wood all help to make an attractive drawing.

Try your hand by copying these, then look around for some to do from life.

An unusual tree, on a windless day, is a good still life subject. In figure 194 the leaves were shaded in, just to try something different – which is to be recommended in most art forms.

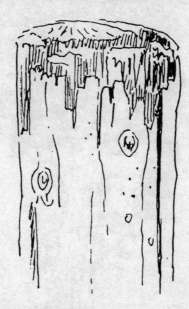

Fig. 193 Try drawing a specific area of an old wooden post, to highlight the detail.

Plants

Notes made of plants and flowers can be very useful for pictures. These are not too hard to draw provided that you look carefully first, as I'm sure you now do. First put down an accurate basic shape then work it into a finished drawing. Always follow the same procedure, then it becomes a good habit. I'm no botanist and quickly forget the proper names of plants and flowers, but this doesn't stop me from admiring and drawing them. Ivy leaves are nice to draw and make pretty compositions; take a look at those in figure 195. You often come across this plant on buildings, trees and old fences. Again, you can add them into pictures with good effect. Start with the basic shape of the leaves, then simply put in the details.

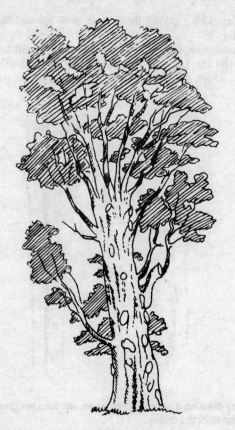

Fig. 194 An unusual tree is always a good still life subject.

Flowers

Generally speaking, flowers are much easier to draw than to paint. If drawn, the first thing is getting down the correct basic shape. Then add in the details of petals, stems and so on. But to paint flowers is a harder task, many colours may be required and dozens of tones. Lady artists shine at this, possibly because they have a more delicate touch than men. A white flower with an orange centre, sketched for this chapter (figure 196), was an ox eye daisy I was told. Take a look at the flowers in figure 197 then try to draw flowers using the same easy system.

Draw flowers by using those around you which may be in a garden, window box, pot, or good photograph.

Grass

Clumps of grass are fine to draw and useful for putting in the foreground of pictures. The grass in figure 198 is of the ordinary lawn sort left to run wild. You guessed right, it's a bit of *my* lawn!

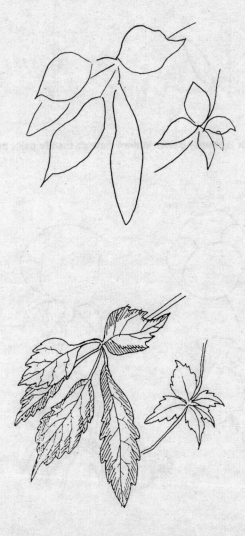

Fig. 195 Ivy leaves make pretty compositions and are nice to draw.

Fig. 196 It is usually easier to draw flowers than to paint them.

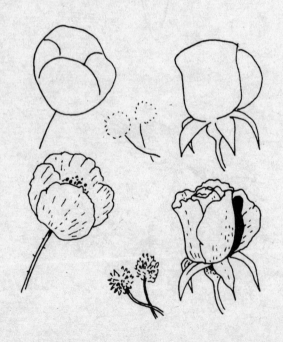

Fig. 197 Try drawing flowers using this easy system.

Fruit

Fruit of all sorts crop up in many still life pictures. I was instantly attracted to great bunches of delicious looking blackberries when out in the countryside, and made the ink drawing in figure 199. Notice how this simple subject can be a study of strong contrasts, black and white. When this picture was finished – I ate them!

Fig. 198 Clumps of grass are useful for putting in the foreground of pictures.

Fig. 199 Many different sorts of fruit apear in still life pictures.

At home

There must be scores of still life subjects for you to draw around you at home. Simple things such as furniture, cooking utensils, food, vases with flowers, your priceless family heirlooms and so on. Many students tend to become bored by sketching everyday objects. If this applies to you please remember that *all* drawing improves your skill and observation.

You could start this exercise by sketching your favourite chair. I chose an old, soft-leather armchair for figure 200 (top), and a rocking chair of the sort which might be my resting place when I have passed my sell-by date!

A grid, as described in Chapter 9, would be of great help to you when attempting still life drawings. Use your grid to help with the perspective of each item you draw. Copy figure 200 for practice.

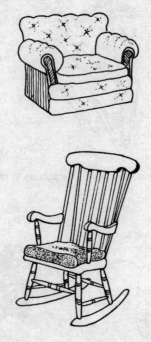

Fig. 200 Drawing furniture improves your observation.

Your car

If you own a car (a stretch limousine perhaps?), you might enjoy drawing it. The problem with sketching motor vehicles (and aircraft) is obtaining straight lines and curves without using expensive draughtsman's equipment. Don't worry. There is a way out for you. Figure 201 shows you how to pop down a basic construction outline using straight lines only. I used a small rule. Notice how the wheel shapes have been suggested. When I was satisfied with the pencil work it was inked over and cleaned up with an eraser. Curved lines are a little tricky to do freehand but you can receive aid by drawing round a saucer, coin or similar object. Copy figure 201.

Assignments
1. Draw a page full of plants from life, if possible.
2. Do the same with old fences, gates or posts.
3. Draw a few studies of objects in your home.

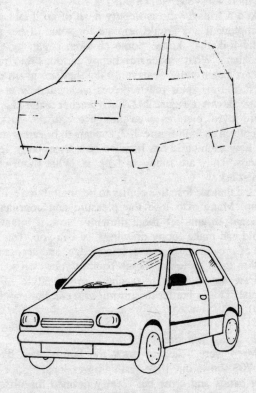

Fig. 201 A car is straight lines and curves.

27
Cartoons For Fun

Most small children are natural cartoonists. They are uninhibited. They draw with bold, confident lines. I wish that many of my adult students would do the same! If you could see the way some mature beginners hesitantly scratch about with a pencil or pen you would laugh – or cry! You, of course, will not be like that, will you? No. Good!

I asked a friend, who is deputy head of an infant school in Northampton, if she would arrange for some of her pupils to draw the folk they knew. Some children began by sketching their teachers. What wonderful, happy cartoons they produced! Infants are much more observant than they are given credit for being. I re-drew their masterpieces as accurately as I could. These are shown in figure 202. Each teacher featured is smiling. They are joyful pictures even though one of the staff, the one that is bottom right in figure 202, appears to be rather menacing. Notice how each child has handled hair style, body, legs, arms and hands. They are funny to look at. What more could any cartoonist ask?

It is sad that we lose this ability to be uninhibited artists as we grow up. Many also lose the pleasure and confidence with which small infants set about drawing. Now, if infants of five years old can make funny drawings, so can you. You have the benefit of greater intelligence, knowledge, and access to books on how to draw cartoons. Think back to your own school days then draw some of your teachers in the style of a child cartoonist. This is harder than it might seem, but should be fun for you!

Begin by being infantile

Children were asked to draw the family they lived with. Figure 203 shows one little girl's impressions. Notice how she left out hands and arms but clearly defined the difference in dress between her father, mother and sisters. Shoes were drawn in a very neat way. I think that this is a delightful drawing. Copy

Fig. 202 Teachers as drawn by infants.

these figures then put in eye pupils, arms and hands. Try to make your cartoons as pleasing as the original.

The youngster who produced the characters for figure 204 used squares to depict the bodies of adults. Because children are small and tend to look up to adults they often draw big feet

Fig. 203 Parents and sisters by an infant cartoonist.

Fig. 204 Drawings of a square family.

which are topped by small heads. All the people drawn were happy looking, even the dog. Re-draw figure 204. Draw in missing bits: feet, arms, hands and noses.

The little boy who drew his father, shown in figure 205, had a good idea of how to sketch features and figures. He left out a finger on one hand, but we shall excuse this small mistake. Could you draw a similar simple cartoon of your father? I'm sure you can. Off you go.

I love the cartoon character created by a girl which I have used for figure 206. She drew circles and whirls to depict the dress, hair and ear rings. Shoes were treated simply. Hands and arms were replaced by wings. This is yet another happy picture. Study this remarkable drawing then have a shot at producing a similar joyful female.

A talented youngster of six made the original drawings for those used in figure 207. Everyone is happy, as usual, including the artist as seen in his self-portrait. I like the way he handled different hair styles. The family cat, Patch, is well drawn. It just needed the far legs to be drawn a bit shorter than those on the near side. Perspective is a problem for infants of all ages up to 90!

What did you learn from infant cartoonists?

You should have learned to draw boldly, confidently and with great freedom of expression. You may have discovered that

Fig. 205 Father drawn by son.

Fig. 206 Is there an angel about?

Fig. 207 A budding cartoonist of six.

basic simple lines can make a pleasing drawing. A different way of jotting down body shapes can work very well. A happy face is easily shown by a smiling mouth. You should have been made aware that each cartoonist has his or her own distinctive style of drawing, that each sees the human being in a slightly different way. Above all, you should have noticed that children draw with great joy and enthusiasm. It shows through. I hope that your happiness will shine from your cartoons.

Assignments
1. Draw child-like cartoons of two people you know.
2. Draw similar cartoons which date back to your childhood.
3. Look at a newspaper or magazine then choose two people to draw in the same way as a child would do them.

28
Doodle Who?

Many people doodle whilst using the telephone, hanging about the office, waiting for somebody to shop or for something to happen on the home front. There are many opportunities to doodle in a normal week. You might be a doodler. I am but my scribbling is under control. Cartoons appear!

Doodle with doodles

If you doodle odd shapes, circles or squares, start to turn them into funny drawings. Figure 209 will show you how to go about this. See how the doodles on the left of the page have been changed into similar shapes but they are now cartoons. I simply made drawings which were suggested by the doodle shape. This is a mite harder than *deliberately* setting out to make all doodles into cartoons straight off. In other words YOU control your particular doodle so that it always begins as a basic shape that is easily turned into a funny drawing. Later you can draw cartoons straight off with a pen as I do. Try copying the finished cartoons in figure 209.

Figure 210 is an example off my telephone pad. It often has more drawings on it than words. You can use your telephone conversations, or intended ones, to inspire ideas. I have a giggle by quickly drawing an off-beat portrait of the person at the other end of my telephone line. The things people say to you can also be used to give birth to cartoon doodles.

Picasso used to doodle on table cloths which then became mighty valuable. Don't be tempted to start this way. Wait a month or two!

Be simple

It would be wise to spend time on trying to keep your cartoons as simple as possible. With this in mind it pays first to draw in pencil, then erase any unnecessary lines before inking in those that are left. By doing this exercise you will soon learn how to use as few lines as possible. The highest form of cartoon

Fig. 209 Doodles changed into cartoons.

Fig. 210 A 'doodled' telephone pad.

art is suggesting form or shape whilst drawing very little. Don't be discouraged if your first attempts do not seem funny to you. It sometimes happens that what may not seem amusing to the creator is to the viewer. If your early work is child-like, be pleased. You are almost there. Don't worry if your efforts are so shaky that they resemble the work of a person under the influence of hard drinking. There are a number of famous artists who have cultivated such a style. As mentioned previously, you have a lot of freedom in this game!

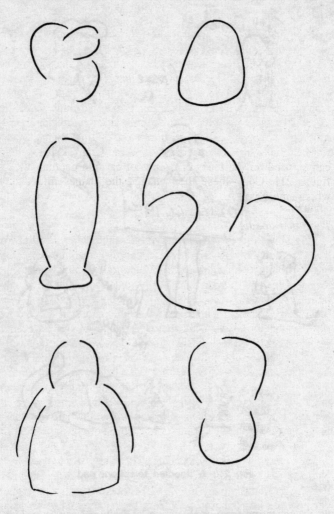

Fig. 211 Turn these doodles into cartoons.

You could try out your brain-children on family or friends. Be positive about practice. Draw cartoons on your small pad every minute that you can. This will quickly help you succeed. Another aid to progress is to force yourself as soon as you can to draw with a pen. Fear of failure sometimes causes beginners to be nervous about straight off ink drawing. Be brave, confident and bold! You can do it.

232

Daily doodle

Now that you have progressed from absent-minded doodling to controlled drawing you can practise daily, every spare moment you get. The more you do the better and faster you will become. Sketch all sorts of subjects as funny cartoons: people, animals, objects. More than one cartoonist has made a fortune from an ability to turn common things into cartoons. The Shoe People is one example, Paddington Bear another. For the moment, however, just concentrate on putting down enough lines to make an amusing drawing. Almost any kind of shape can be used for the faces or figures of cartoon people. Look at figure 211. Copy these then change the shapes into figures which amuse you.

The super doodle

It is now time for you to move on to the super doodle. You have learned how to convert odd doodles into cartoons, then how deliberately to draw cartoons as doodles. Now I want you to go to the next stage: fast, controlled, casual cartoons. Just before writing this piece I grabbed a small sketch pad, went outside my house, looked at people around and then jotted down my cartoon impressions of them. The results can be seen in figure 212. I timed this little exercise: I looked at each victim for about half a minute before drawing him in, say, ten to fifteen seconds. The whole process took all of ten minutes. Cartoon production can be quick fun! Note the whistling postman, the tall thin man, the dog with a plume-like tail. There were no ladies about at the time. I'm sure you will appreciate how these cartoons are not very far removed from true life drawings. Yours can be way out if you like. Copy these for practice.

I drew the faces shown in figure 212 in my own natural style. Notice the way eyes, noses and other features can be depicted. Remember that there are no rules. You have freedom to express your people just the way you want them. They can have huge heads, small bodies, gigantic feet or can be like stick people. Anything goes so long as it's funny to look at and resembles the real thing. To illustrate this last point I took the examples used in figure 212 then re-drew them. I simply exaggerated what had been drawn previously. Look at figure 213. Notice how I have made more of some things. Heads have been enlarged to emphasize the expressions of the postman and the child, for example. The dog was given a larger tail and a smug look. These sketches took a little longer due to thinking time – all of one minute per drawing! Copy these.

Try drawing from life for yourself. You can look at your subjects for two whole minutes then spend one minute drawing each. I spoil you but I'm sure you're worth it!

The human face is the hardest feature to learn how to cartoon although it is not all that difficult. If you play about with a pen and scribble noses, eyes, mouths and general head shapes you will quickly discover the type of thing that you find funny to look at. By all means copy my work, but never forget that your own hidden style could be better than mine. While we are all

Fig. 212 Simple super doodles from life.

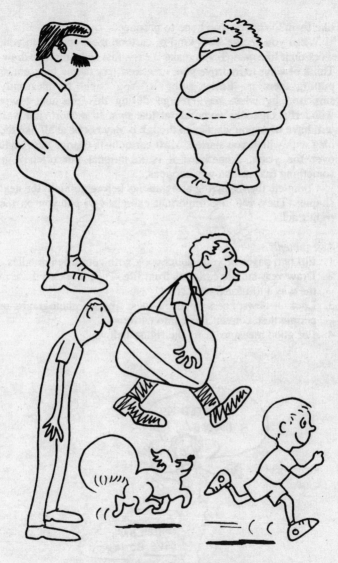

Fig. 213 Super doodles exaggerated.

influenced to some degree by other artists, naturally we must all come up with our own thing. You can't force this to happen; it just evolves painlessly. Ask yourself what sort of drawings seem the most amusing to you. Which ones do you like? Why do you like them? What do you hope to produce?

When you decide what kind of cartoon most appeals to you, work on it like mad. Try to make it easy, fast and simple to draw. Think of ways to improve your creations. Try taking lines out or putting them in. Enjoy doing it. You could be pleasantly surprised by what may emerge during this practice. Many wonderful creations come about like this. In a short time you will have what you want even though it may not be at all like the idea with which you started. Most cartoonists change their style over the years. Sometimes it is intentional but often it is something that just slowly happens.

Complete the following assignments before going to the next chapter. They, too, are important exercises to put you on the right track.

Assignments
1. Fill two pages of your sketchbook with controlled doodles.
2. Draw very simple cartoons from life. Then work on these in the way I did for figure 213.
3. Look at newspapers or magazines. Choose photographs of people then convert these into cartoons.
4. For good measure, copy the figure below.

29
Express Expressions

In this chapter I shall show you how to draw the correct expressions on the faces of your cartoon characters. You can sometimes tell the mood of fellow humans by the way they set their facial features. Some folk, however, hide their feelings behind a dead-pan face. Others give away their thoughts and moods. What can we see in another person's face? There are scores of moods reflected in many different permutations. Happiness, sadness, worry, shyness, cunning, anger, joy, surprise and lots of other emotions. A cartoonist simply exaggerates what is seen so that a reader instantly knows what the cartoon character feels.

Important lines

Because you are most likely to be a happy person I shall first show you how to draw happy faces. The mouth line clearly shows when someone is in a happy mood; it curves upwards. The eyebrows may stay still; more often they arch or tighten up slightly. Have a look at figure 215. Notice how a smile can be extended into great mirth or joy, as in the bottom sketches. You will see that eyes can help to determine mood. They can seem to become round, or narrow, or may even close. There can be tears of joy flying about as well! Copy the examples in this figure with a pen.

A gloomy facial expression is the opposite of a happy one. The mouth lines go *down* while the eyebrows either remain up, stay fairly straight or turn down towards the nose. Anger or fury are progressions of gloom. These are the lower illustrations in figure 216. Copy these cartoon faces.

Invent your own head!

Scribble down a page or two of oval shapes to use as cartoon heads. Then play about with a pencil. Begin with a frontal face. Look at figure 217 to see how this is done. You can practise by drawing frontal heads, profile ones (from the side) and then in-

Fig. 215　Draw happy faces.

Fig. 216　How to depict unhappy faces.

between ones, as in figure 218. For the latter, pencil in a dotted guideline, as shown, to help position the main features; then construct a face from that.

Figure 219 shows different cartoon faces in profile. I usually begin by drawing in big noses for my fictional men and small ones for ladies. See how I have drawn each feature. Then have a go at drawing your versions. Figure 220, of semi-frontal faces, is worth studying before you copy it. Now you have basic face shapes from which to work or develop. You can experiment with oblongs, circles, squares or whatever. Remember, however, that a cartoon must be recognizable as the real subject.

Fig. 217 A frontal cartoon face.

Put on your funny face

Before attempting other moods and feelings I will give you a good tip which will help you to capture different expressions. Use a mirror and yourself! It is important to relax and observe yourself carefully. You will learn an awful lot by doing a spot of acting, watching what your face does when it reflects a mood or

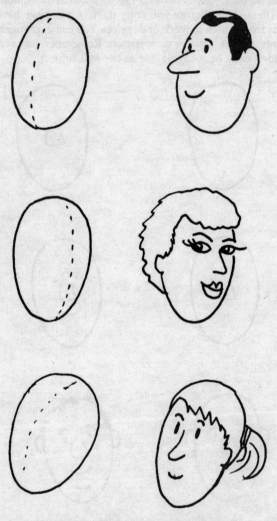

Fig. 218 Construct your cartoon faces.

Fig. 219 Faces in profile.

Fig. 220 A collection of expressions.

emotion. You may want to do this when you are alone, or you might be a happy extrovert who can perform before a huge audience!

Your acting could be so brilliant that you are tempted into thoughts of a career on the stage. My advice to 9½ out of 10 of you is to dismiss any such ideas. Remember Noël Coward's song 'Don't put your daughter on the stage, Mrs Worthington!' For most of us who must go on the stage it is wise to think in terms of scrubbing it daily for a steady wage!

Friends have told me that when I'm drawing cartoons my face registers the expressions I put on my characters. Strangers who witness this amazing scene tend to think that I am quite mad!

The next part of this fun exercise is to jot down quickly the important lines you see when you are pulling faces at yourself.

Start with the easy expressions, happiness and gloom, then

progress to anxiety, surprise, disdain, bewilderment, and any others that you might fancy. The drawings in figure 220 cover some of the expressions mentioned. Close examination of many published cartoons will help you quickly to get the hang of this skill.

Helpful hair

A person's hair can help to suggest what the owner is like. Untidy hair, extra long hair, neat hair and hair standing on end each give strong clues. Take another look at figures 219 and 220 and then copy those examples. Notice how filling in with ink has been used. When drawing hair styles aim to get what you want with as few lines as possible. It pays, over and over again, to simplify cartoons. Do you remember how children draw hair?

You may have noticed how cartoonists draw young ladies. Some are drawn as glamorous pin-ups with exotic heads of hair while others are sketched to raise a laugh. It's we fellows who are mostly drawn as ugly, ape-like creatures. This observation gave rise to the cartoon and caption in figure 221.

Fig. 221 "Look, Gran! An ape has escaped!"

Fig. 222 Give hats to your characters.

Put a lid on it

Now that you have drawn heads think about putting lids on them. Hats for men are not so popular as they once were though cartoon characters often have them. Headgear is more frequently seen on ladies. It comes in all shapes and sizes. You can invent your own if you wish. Take a glance at those drawn for figure 222. Copy them and then design a couple of your own.

Choose your eyes

You should now practise drawing eyes for your cartoon characters. Each artist seems to have a pet way of depicting eyes. It's easier to portray an attractive young lady by exaggerating her eyes as in figures 219 and 220. You will see in those examples that the size of the eyes has been increased and long eyelashes are tacked on where the character requires them. Some cartoon people have tiny dots for eyes and others have lidded peepers. You should play about with a page full of different kinds of eyes, then concentrate on the type which you like the best. Look back at some of the earlier figures for examples of different cartoon eyes.

Fig. 223 Two different face shapes.

Face types

The shape of a face can suggest the type of person it belongs to. Cartoonists tend to portray a simple person as having little forehead, with the eyes set high up. Intelligence, on the other hand, is often depicted by giving the person an egg-shaped head, with the eyes positioned low down and hidden behind glasses. Figure 223 illustrates these techniques. In actual fact this theory is nonsense, but it works in cartoons. There is no end to the range of face shapes that you may use for your creations. Some cartoonists have characters with square heads. You are free to do your own thing.

An average sort of face can be suggested by drawing a simple oval shape and putting in the mouth as a straight line. Making the face expressionless is an aid a cartoonist might use to show a straight or stooge character, a listener, a silent witness or a bystander. Figure 224 will give you an idea of this type of character. Copy these examples.

245

Fig. 224 Neutral expressions.

Assignments
1. Draw cartoon faces of both sexes expressing the following moods: surprise, worry, anger, laughter and shock. If in doubt, use yourself and a mirror, or enlist a friend.
2. Draw two different hair styles for men and women. Draw two people wearing hats.
3. Draw a cartoon containing an angry person shouting at a worried looking character of either sex.
4. Copy the end-of-chapter super doodle saga from now on.

30
Funny Figures

Drawing faces and expressions is the hardest part of creating cartoons. Now it's easy. You need to draw a cartoon body for the head that you've already designed. Bodies, like faces, come in a wide variety of sizes and shapes and abilities to get into trouble: tall, thin, fat, short, round, angular and combinations of these. You can convert almost any odd shape into a cartoon body. Study figure 226. See how easy it is? If you start off with a basic shape which is already like a human body then the job is even easier. Some artists use the shape they have invented for all their characters. I prefer to base mine on real people; then I stretch or contract my first drawing of them as required. Experiment until you find what suits you.

Copy the examples in figure 226. Then draw in the missing heads. Try to work straight off with a pen. Move next to figure 227. These are the pre-formed bodies rather than odd shapes. See how I have drawn footwear, limbs and hands. It isn't always necessary to draw five-finger hands; you can get away with just three or four due to the wide degree of artistic licence allowed to all cartoonists. Draw all the figures and then jot in the heads. The two lower figures have their backs to you but you could make the faces so they look left or right rather than just drawing the backs of their heads.

Perhaps it is just as well that the majority of cartoons feature clothed characters. A cartoonist needs to keep an eye on current fashions, but not to the extent required of commercial artists or designers. Some cartoonists tend to draw their men in ageless, nondescript suits or clothes (a bit like my wardrobe!). Readers spend only a split-second looking at cartoons so the clothes characters wear are not all that important. When you churn out drawings from life you can't go wrong because nowadays everybody is dressed so differently. There is an amazing range of garments. It is not like the bad old days when the working class all dressed alike as did, for their parts, the middle and the so-called upper classes. Teenagers tend to follow their own fashions while the rest of us put on what we like.

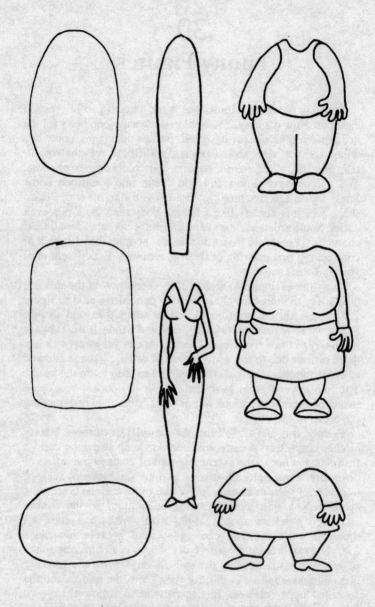

Fig. 226 How to turn odd shapes into cartoon bodies.

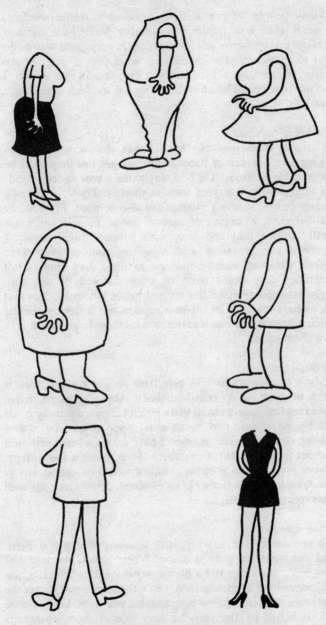

Fig. 227 Draw these headless bodies.

249

Many people wear a uniform: policemen, traffic wardens, soldiers, etc. You might try dressing your own cartoon characters in uniforms just for practice. A very good way to do so is to record in your sketchbook what people you see are wearing at the time. Figure 228 will give you an idea of this. I used my size 2 paint brush and drawing ink to block in the black areas.

Bunches of bananas

Cartoon characters can have hands drawn with fingers looking like a bunch of bananas or sausages but they must be recognizable as hands! The best way to learn how to draw hands and fingers is to use your own as models. Those of friends, spouses or unsuspecting victims can also be used. Figures 229 and 230 show examples of cartoon hands. Female hands are usually drawn thin and long with painted finger nails. A cartoonist can get away with sketching four or even three fingers. Children usually manage to draw five fingers but sometimes they don't quite fit onto the end of the arm. Beginners tend to make fingers and hands too small. Not that this matters much in an off-beat cartoon but it does make the drawing harder. It is much easier to draw them large than it is to draw them small.

Big feet

Many cartoonists love to give their people gigantic feet. It seems to work, as do boat-like shoes. Anything seems to go. One exception appears to be that elegant ladies are usually given high-heeled shoes. Old battle-axes, poor dears, are drawn wearing clog-type monstrosities. I have drawn a small selection of shoes for figure 231. Copy these. Then invent a few designs of your own. I once asked a group of would-be cartoonists to sketch each other's footwear as cartoons. They came up with some spectacular designs.

Action figures

If you are new to drawing, stick figures can help you. First, think out what the body is doing. Where should the legs and arms be? If you don't know the answer ask a friend to pose, use a mirror or look at photographs. Draw the stick figure to get the pose; then thicken it out to portray what you want. Study figure 232. It helps, by the way, to have one or more characters showing feelings as well. Their simple reactions to shock,

Fig. 228 Record what some people wear.

Fig. 229 Draw hands like bunches of bananas.

pleasure, fear, surprise, joy and so on can be deliberately exaggerated.

Body language

Become aware of what people do. Be a person watcher. Notice how people sit, stand, walk, talk and so on. We are told that most of us give away our intentions by body language. Get into the habit of jotting down a quick sketch or even a stick figure based on what you see. This is good fun, especially if the model is unaware of what you are doing.

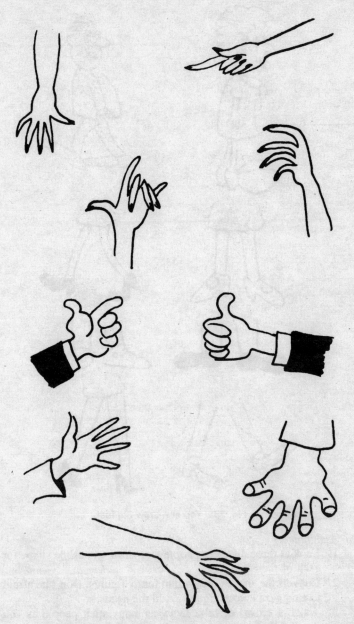

Fig. 230 See how female hands can be drawn.

Fig. 231 You can draw big feet.

Assignments
1. Look at three different people then draw an outline shape for each of their bodies.
2. Convert the shapes drawn into funny figures. Don't be afraid to exaggerate your figures. Add the heads.
3. Watch a crowd of folk. Draw as many stick people as you can and then turn them into funny cartoons.

Fig. 232 Stick figures can help you.

31
Feature Creatures

Cheep, cheep

In this chapter we shall feature creatures as funny cartoons. I have always found that birds are simple to create in a comical way. I begin by scribbling away with a pencil at the basic shape of a bird until something emerges. Figure 234 will show you how I construct a bird cartoon. Notice that the body and head start as oval forms; the beak, wings and tail are roughly triangular. A large eye is drawn in. When I am satisfied with a pencil sketch I refine it with details: the eye pupil, a suggestion of feathers, the mouth line and then the feet. Lastly I go over my drawing with a size 0.1 pen and, once it is dry, rub out the pencil marks. A new cartoon is born!

Before you tackle birds, animals or fish remember the great importance of *constructing* every drawing that you do, *starting* from the correct basic shape of the particular creature you have chosen. I can't stress too much how vital this is. A beginner cartoonist's worst mistake is to imagine, or indeed to look at, what they are drawing and then try to start on some detail such as a beak. This is the wrong way to go about the job because you are likely to get it out of proportion and, very shortly, the whole thing becomes a mess. If, however, you *build* the basic construction lines as your first step, the rest becomes very easy – just a matter of popping in the details. Apply this simple rule to all your art and you will make rapid progress. You will soon surprise yourself, your friends, and maybe even your bank manager!

You are now ready to copy the birds in figure 234. There are more feathered friends drawn for figure 235: a tatty looking song bird, a sad-faced duck, a bird of prey, a cross-eyed woodpecker (high-speed drilling must be hard on their beaks and bones) and a little swallow. Think out the basic shapes for the last two first; then copy the lot. You don't have to stick to what I have done. Do your own thing!

Fig. 234 How to construct a bird cartoon.

Fig. 235 Draw these birds.

Fig. 236 Build dog cartoons.

Dogs galore

"Man's best friend" was always a thought applied to dogs, but now I have my doubts. There are an awful lot of badly trained, badly handled guard dogs about. Some of these lethal

Fig. 237 Some of the many breeds of dog.

animals are man's worst enemy! The average house dog, thank goodness, is usually a happy, harmless pet which lends itself to cartooning. We shall use our skill on him. Study figure 236. See how I have drawn the basic shape of each dog before refining it into a finished cartoon. Note how eyes and mouth, as in people, can denote mood. The little hairy dog was drawn with short pen strokes. Fur texture was further suggested by dots and dashes.

The many breeds of dog give us cartoonists a wide choice of subject. Figure 237 shows a few of them. The bull terrier at the

Fig. 238 Draw comical cats.

top of the page was inspired after watching an old film of Oliver Twist. It stuck in my mind for some reason. The retriever (middle sketch) was given a sloppy but friendly look which reflects the temperament of these pets. (I hope no reader has been bitten by one!) I put a crown on the head of the King Charles spaniel. It was a pretty obvious thing to do but we can't all be brilliant all the time!

Comical cats

The cartoons drawn for figure 238 were not far removed from life. I simply worked on the eyes and mouth. Small changes

Fig. 239 Cartoon alley cats.

262

Fig. 240 Draw large animals as cartoons.

sometimes give the best results for me. If your natural style is
off-beat or wildly exaggerated stick to it; don't be influenced by
my work. Beginners, by the way, often try too hard. This results
in tight, over-crowded drawings with the humour blotted out by
detail. The aim, once again, is to produce a funny picture. Copy
the cats in figure 238.

I invented an alley cat for figure 239. It is a bit cunning but
interesting (which reminds me of a former lady friend!). Did
you know that if a cat approaches you with its tail held straight
up it is giving you a welcome sign? Now I know this I always
stop to give a gentle pat and a few kind words. I know that you
will do the same. See what you can do with the examples in
figure 239.

Draw big ones

Animals are popular subjects for greetings cards, children's books, cartoon films and many other commercial projects. I reckon almost every known creature is worthy of a funny drawing. It is possible to invent new animals. ET, of movie fame, is one good example. Large animals are perhaps slightly easier to sketch than small ones. The horse in figure 240 was deliberately drawn with shaky lines to show you what you can get away with doing. I made the legs rather like those of a pantomime horse just for fun. Pigs are quite comical to look at so making them into cartoons is relatively simple. In my example I worked on the face but left the body more or less life-like. The giraffe was treated in a similar fashion. Again, small changes work for my style.

Assignments

1. From a photograph draw a cartoon elephant.
2. Draw a cartoon of the family pet or that of a neighbour.
3. Cartoon an owl, a pigeon, or a crow.

32
Draw Funny Things

The ability to turn ordinary things into amusing cartoons is easy to learn. It need be no more than an extension of controlled doodling. The trick is to think out simple ideas and then apply them to chosen subjects.

I used a leek, an onion and an old carrot for the examples in figure 242 I turned the leek upside down to create a cartoon character; the onion was placed on its side (which suggested a comic fish to my cartoon brain); the carrot was moved around until the funny figure evolved for the bottom sketch. By using this method it should be possible to change any object into a cartoon. Try it for yourself, but don't try too hard! Just let it happen. Copy figure 242. Use your own ideas on the faces.

Cartoons can be teaching aids

I use cartoons in all my writing as I have found that using them makes the text more light-hearted, and that it often provides a good way of making a point.

When I once worked on health promotion in primary schools I was required to give a session on "Healthy Hearts". I showed children how to draw a cartoon heart then asked them to draw their versions showing different physical activities which were good for the heart. Some of the ideas I used are shown in figure 243. Notice how simple drawing works: a big face drawn in the heart shape with small limbs and enough to suggest what sport was involved. The female hearts, of course, were pretty.

On other school projects I used popular cartoons to put over information. Children always found these sessions fun. It was sometimes difficult to get them to stop in order to give me a break! The same technique was used when teaching management, communication and public relations skills to adults. Cartoons really are fun!

I once had an office job that required urgent action from others in order to get my job done. Many notes and memoranda were sent out but when there was an undue delay or nothing

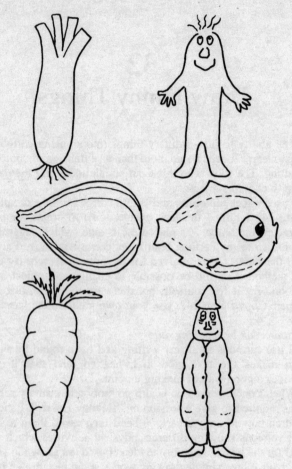

Fig. 242 Draw funny things.

done, I would draw a funny face or cartoon on a reminder. This almost always worked. I would receive a friendly telephone call followed by prompt attention. You might have a job which could be improved by a quick cartoon. Humour is priceless.

Take things literally

I set about thinking how I could make books into cartoons. Figure 244 resulted. The two top sketches were my first thoughts. They are pretty obvious jokes: I just popped on to the book cover a face which was appropriate to the title. This idea was extended in the other drawings by having the books *do* something which used the title literally. This is a trick worth remembering, and one used by many humorists. Draw your version of figure 244.

Fig. 243 Healthy heart cartoons.

Fig. 244 How to make books into cartoons.

Everything is usable

An old walking boot inspired the cartoon face in figure 245. See how I used the shape of the boot to form a funny face. The toe cap became a silly grin and the tongue a nose; eyes were then added along with a hat. With a little practice you can soon become reasonably good at this skill. You will have seen many examples of this craft used on commercial television to promote or sell various goods. There have been animated boxes, peas, loaves, bottles and scores of other usually inanimate objects. Now that you are a budding cartoonist you will see similar advertisements with new eyes. Knowledge of your subject can make you critical of poor work but you will learn from the good stuff.

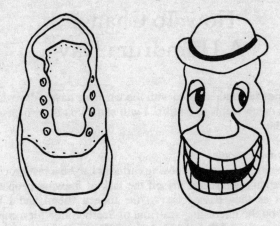

Fig. 245 Change a boot into a face.

Assignments
1. Draw a cartoon each from a pear, a tree trunk and a banana.
2. Make a cartoon based on a book on flying.
3. Look at figure 246 then think out and draw a possibility for the next exciting episode.

Fig. 246

269

33

How To Change
A Humdrum Day

We may feel rather bored with life when we have a day where nothing much seems to happen. I will show you how to change such a day.

Create funny people

As mentioned earlier, drawing cartoons can be a fast process. To prove this point I set myself the task of drawing people as cartoons as they passed by. At the time a friend and I had stopped on the interesting sea-front of Scarborough for a cup of tea. I carried my A5 sketch pad and a 2B pencil. I used a well-tried method of working: I looked at my victim for as long as possible. In most cases this was a matter of seconds, but even during this time I always took in the key points of their overall appearance: their clothes, footwear, hair fashion, facial characteristics and their physical build. I then jotted down a basic figure with an exaggerated hair style and a rough face. My total concentration went on into quickly producing a cartoon character from what I had seen. I soon discovered that people on the move did not re-appear for me to have a second look at them. There was just one chance at this lark.

Figure 247 is of six quite ordinary looking holiday makers. The girls were, in fact, quite pretty but I did not make them so in the finished cartoons. What would they say if they knew? The object was to make them *funny* to look at. The more beautiful a victim is, the greater the challenge to me, and, I hope, to you. Notice how I have drawn the various hair fashions, footwear and clothes. See how I have used shading to give a little depth to a line drawing. Dark colours were suggested by close diagonal lines. Try this when copying the people in this figure or doing some more of your own.

It is marvellous to see all the weird and wonderful outfits which people wear today. It is a great help to cartoonists when

270

Fig. 247 Cartoon people on holiday.

everybody wears something different from their fellows. The folk who were used for figure 248 are an example of this. Note the old lady clad in a thick woolly jersey and long skirt; this was surprising gear to wear on a very hot summer day. See how I drew the man who had his sweater tied round his fat neck.

It is easy to draw varied hair styles if they are depicted in a simple way. Pay attention to how I do this.

I cartoon-captured a man here at Scarborough who I thought was typical of an elderly North Country gentleman, although he might have hailed from Brighton for all I knew! He is on the bottom right in figure 249. Note his flat cap, along with the ancient coat. A passing street cleaner I caught contemplating

271

Fig. 248 A few of the wonderful outfits people wear.

who knows what. The young lady, top left, had long beautiful hair (see how it looks now), shapely legs, black tights, a bulky jacket worn over a short, pleated skirt and huge boots. She was a ready-made cartoon. The other lady drawn had a superb head of hair which I quickly messed up with a controlled scribble. (My own thatch is thinning so I'm jealous!) I was working at great speed, chuckling as I worked, but my mug of tea had gone cold. Did it serve me right? No, I am so glad you agree with me!

Another ready-made living cartoon character in the shape of the lady, lower right, in figure 250, appeared then disappeared before I could start to draw her. My companion and I, however, talked over what she had been wearing. Then I drew the cartoon you see. A young lady who was looking for someone was my next victim. Take note how I drew her hair and skirt blowing in the wind. My next subject was a doleful-looking dog with its owner who sported a colourful shirt. A boy running caught my eye, as did the girl walking away from where I sat. In forty minutes thirty two people were drawn. Have fun copying all the illustrations of these lovely people.

You need not go out to practise

A seaside resort offers a wide range of humanity to play about with, but what if you are stuck indoors, the rain is tipping down – with your nose trying to follow suit – and you don't have the bus fare to go anywhere? What can you do to brighten your humdrum day? "Quite a lot" is my answer! You can create

Fig. 249 My passing victims.

Fig. 250 Some folk are living cartoons.

Fig. 251 Draw the cast of a third rate movie.

your own world of imaginary cartoon characters based on any real ones you might see from your window, doorway, or on television. To test this out I forced myself to watch an old movie on TV. Take a peep at figure 251 to see what I did to two of the leading ladies and other members of the cast. There was a strident-voiced, irritating child actor in the film. I was at a loss

Fig. 252 Cartoons inspired by newspapers.

to know what sex it was but did decide that it deserved a regular smack with a wet sock. My drawings of the actors in this classic flop improved them no end, but I won't be visiting Hollywood just yet! Isn't being a cartoonist great fun? Draw your version of the film cast.

Let your newspaper inspire you

A fit of madness can sometimes help a cartoonist produce funny drawings. This condition gave birth to a few wild cartoons which you can see in figure 252. At the time I had opened my daily newspaper to look at the pictures. No, not because I could not read – I simply wanted to turn some people into funny cartoons. My first choice was a very famous member of our Royal family. I will not mention who it is. I might not receive a full English breakfast in the Tower of London! I next attacked, with a pencil, an up-market young lady who had been photographed at a high society bash. The state of her dress reminded me to think about buying a new second-hand shirt for Christmas. Lastly I came across a picture of a particularly handsome man. He was far too good-looking for his own good. I soon changed him! See how my normal style of drawing altered as the madness took me over. I loved every second of it. Try to become slightly mentally unhinged when you copy figure 252.

Assignments
1. Go out to any place busy with people. Then draw six of them who you see as funny cartoons.
2. Draw four cartoon characters based on some you see on your TV.
3. Choose three newspaper photographs of people; then radically change them into funny cartoons.

34
Draw Your Own Greetings Cards

Designing greetings cards in order to sell them to commercial concerns is a tough, highly competitive business. Many greetings card companies have their own artists and those that do not tend to pay poor rates. You can, however, easily produce your own cartoon cards to cover any event. Your family or friends will, I assure you, be pleased to receive one of your little gems on a special occasion. There are numerous days honoured by greetings cards: Mothers', Fathers' and Grandparents' days; Christmas, New Year and Easter; Valentine, birthday, wedding, birth, retirement, promotion and congratulations – just to mention a few. There are many outlets for your cartoon talents.

Materials to use

You can draw your designs on thick drawing paper, artist's board, or good cardboard. Use your normal drawing pen for the sketches. Your finished work can be enhanced by the use of a spot of colour. Use coloured pencils, highlighters, water colours or poster paints.

Look through old cards to decide what size you will use. Open one out then measure it. Notice which side the cover design is on and which page has the caption, if any. Cut out a similar size blank card and fold it in half. (A ruler is handy for this. With it you can first score a folding line down the middle of your paper using a sharp point such as a steel knitting needle or an awl.) Remember to keep the front cover with the fold on your left before you begin, lightly, to pencil in a design. Ink it in when you are satisfied.

An easy start for you

The Christmas season heralds the exchange of millions of greetings cards. There are many possible subjects to cartoon but a particularly easy one is snowmen. This is little more than a controlled doodle. You could draw a cartoon snowman with one

of your eyes closed. Look at figure 254. This idea came to me
out of the proverbial blue. I quickly jotted it down. The caption
could just as appropriately have been placed inside the card.
This design is ideal for a tall, slim Christmas card. The finished
drawing could be improved by the use of colour. A little blue
added to indicate shadow, a grey winter sky, a few red-nosed
snowmen and that is about it. There is another snowman, with
offspring, for you to look at in figure 255. Also included is a

Fig. 254 Snowmen are easy to draw.

cartoon robin which is a very popular bird for Christmas cards. Copy figures 254 and 255 for practice.

Visual jokes, the sort that do not require a caption, are very popular world-wide because no language translations are needed. Figure 256 is my example of this type of gag. See how everything has been drawn with as few lines as possible. A seasonal greeting could easily be put inside. Re-draw this one with your own characters.

Fig. 255 Aim for simple drawing.

Fig. 256 A visual cartoon.

Cartoon animals

You may have noticed that scores of greetings card designers use animals to put over a message. Horses, dogs, cats, mice, reindeer and many other species regularly crop up. Figure 257 was drawn to show you how one idea can be used at least twice. You can often do this. Ideas beget ideas; the more that you think of, the more that flit into your mind. Take note of how I have used a few short pen strokes to suggest fur in the cat. Draw your versions of these ideas.

I sometimes forget a friend's birthday but try to make up for my weakness by sending an original cartoon to bridge the gap. Figure 258 is a copy of one that I sent to a chum several weeks after the event. On the original card I put the lower caption on the inside. This cartoon elephant is another simple sketch. Try drawing your idea of a gentle giant.

I have used the giraffe frequently in cartoons. It has a funny natural shape so it is easy to turn into a comic drawing. Figure

Fig. 257 Animal cartoons are popular.

SORRY I FORGOT......

YOUR.... ER.... WOTSIT

Fig. 258 Are you late with birthday cards?

259 was drawn for a friend's wedding. See how I drew the female giraffe slightly smaller than the male. I also added in eyelashes. A similar idea could be used for congratulating a birth. This would simply require drawing in a baby giraffe. Why not try it yourself?

People inspire cartoon ideas

I have previously mentioned how people can inspire cartoon ideas. It might be something they say, do, or wear. An example of this happened on my cartoon course when one student bought a new hat for herself. The headgear gave me the idea of a witch.

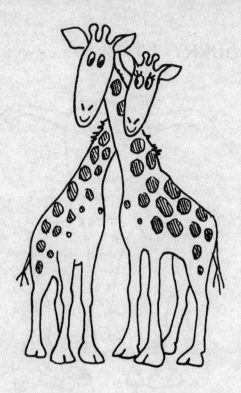

CONGRATULATIONS

Fig. 259 Animal cartoons are easy to think out.

The lady concerned, bless her, was far removed from being a witch. She was, in fact, very witty, generous and talented. The original thought evolved into a funny scene of the sort I draw just to amuse my friends. Thus figure 260 is the result of a nice lady buying a straw hat! Isn't it strange how the mind works? This cartoon also shows how you can add words to make a joke or put over information. Now draw your cartoon witch.

Fig. 260 A cartoon based on a real person.

Now you have come to the end of this book I hope that you are eager to continue your hobby as a good all-round artist. Thank you for being my student. The best of luck to you.